MAPPING SKILLS WITH GOOGLE EARTH™

Mapping Skills Series

Written by Paul Bramley

GRADES 3-5

Classroom Complete Press
P.O. Box 19729
San Diego, CA 92159
Tel: 1-800-663-3609 / Fax: 1-800-663-3608
Email: service@classroomcompletepress.com

www.classroomcompletepress.com

ISBN-13: 978-1-55319-550-4

Critical Thinking Skills

Mapping Skills with Google Earth™

Skills for Critical Thinking		Basics of Map Reading	Latitude, Longitude and Times Zones	Mapping Geographical Features	Mapping Cultural Features	Map Your Country	Map the World
		Reading Comprehension					
LEVEL 1 Remembering	• Match	✓		✓	✓		
	• Show or Label			✓		✓	✓
	• List Information				✓	✓	
	• Recall Details		✓	✓	✓	✓	✓
	• Find Information	✓	✓	✓	✓	✓	✓
LEVEL 2 Understanding	• Describe & Compare	✓	✓	✓	✓		
	• Summarize				✓		
	• Explain	✓		✓	✓		
	• Select		✓			✓	✓
LEVEL 3 Applying	• Organize Information		✓		✓	✓	✓
	• Interview						
	• Apply	✓	✓	✓	✓	✓	✓
	• Utilize Altnerative Research Tools (Google Earth)	✓	✓	✓	✓	✓	✓
LEVEL 4 Analysing	• Conclude		✓		✓		✓
	• Analyze		✓	✓	✓		✓
LEVEL 5 Evaluating	• Evaluate			✓	✓		✓
	• Compare		✓	✓	✓		✓
LEVEL 6 Creating	• Design			✓	✓	✓	✓
	• Create			✓	✓	✓	✓

Based on Bloom's Taxonomy

Contents

TEACHER GUIDE

STUDENT HANDOUTS

Assessment Rubric

Mapping Skills with Google Earth™

Student's Name: ____________________ Assignment: ____________________ Level: __________

	Level 1	Level 2	Level 3	Level 4
Understanding Concepts	Demonstrates a limited understanding of the concepts. Requires teacher intervention	Demonstrates a basic understanding of the concepts. Requires some teacher intervention	Demonstrates a good understanding of the concepts. Requires minimal teacher intervention	Demonstrates a thorough understanding of the concepts. Requires no teacher intervention
Responses to the Text	Expresses responses to the text with limited effectiveness, inconsistently supported by proof from the text	Expresses responses to the text with some effectiveness, supported by some proof from the text	Expresses responses to the text with appropriate skills, supported with appropriate proof	Expresses thorough and complete responses to the text, supported by concise and effective proof from the text
Application of Own Interests	Interprets and applies various concepts in the text with few, unrelated details and incorrect analysis	Interprets and applies various concepts in the text with some detail, but with some inconsistent analysis	Interprets and applies various concepts in the text with appropriate detail and analysis	Effectively interprets and applies various concepts in the text with consistent, clear and effective detail and analysis

STRENGTHS:

WEAKNESSES:

NEXT STEPS:

Teacher Guide

Our resource has been created for ease of use by both TEACHERS and STUDENTS alike.

Introduction

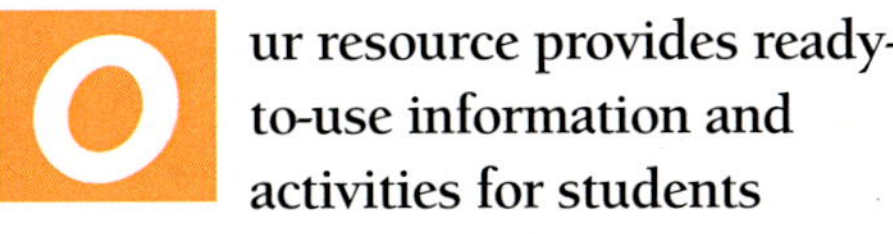
Our resource provides ready-to-use information and activities for students in grades 3 to 5. It builds upon previously learned mapping skills such as elements of maps, how to draw and label maps, and the purposes of maps. This series expands on that knowledge as it starts off with a review on the basics of map reading. Following this, students will learn about lines of latitude, longitude, and time zones. Then, students will learn the differences between mapping geographical and cultural features, and the importance of both. Finally, students will expand their knowledge by mapping their country and finally the world. Comprised of reading passages, student activities and mini posters, our resource can be used effectively for whole-class, small group and independent study.

How Is Our Resource Organized?

STUDENT HANDOUTS

Reading passages and **activities** (*in the form of reproducible worksheets*) make up the majority of our resource. The reading passages present important grade-appropriate information and concepts related to the topic. Embedded in each passage are **Google Earth™ activities**. Students will apply the concepts they have learned with the use of technology. Download Google Earth™ at ***earth.google.com***, then follow the instructions to install it. You will need to be connected to the internet.

For each reading passage there are **BEFORE YOU READ** activities and **AFTER YOU READ** activities.

- The BEFORE YOU READ activities prepare students for reading by setting a purpose for reading. They stimulate background knowledge and experience, and guide students to make connections between what they know and what they will learn. Important concepts and vocabulary from the chapters are also presented.
- The AFTER YOU READ activities check students' comprehension of the concepts presented in the reading passage and extend their learning. Students are asked to give thoughtful consideration of the reading passage through creative and evaluative short-answer questions, research, and extension activities.

An additional **Map Activity** is included in every chapter, allowing students to apply the concepts that they have learned. The **Assessment Rubric** (*page 4*) is a useful tool for evaluating students' responses to many of the activities in our resource. The **Comprehension Quiz** (*page 42*) can be used for either a follow-up review or assessment at the completion of the unit.

PICTURE CUES

This resource contains three main types of pages, each with a different purpose and use. A **Picture Cue** at the top of each page shows, at a glance, what the page is for.

Teacher Guide
- Information and tools for the teacher

Student Handouts
- Reproducible task sheets and drill sheets

Easy Marking™ Answer Key
- Answers for student activities

EASY MARKING™ ANSWER KEY

Marking students' worksheets is fast and easy with our **Answer Key**. Answers are listed in columns – just line up the column with its corresponding worksheet, as shown, and see how every question matches up with its answer!

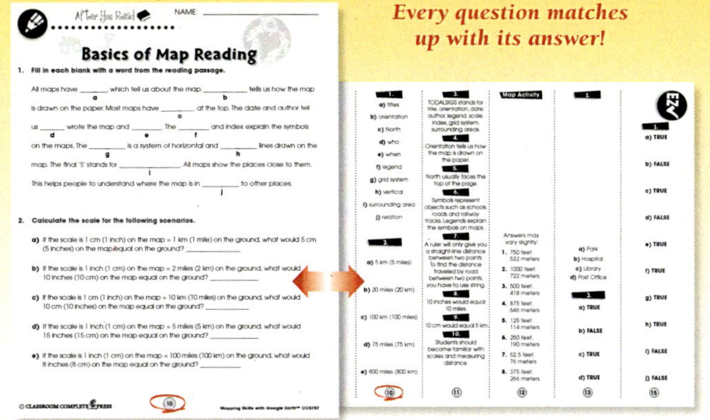

Bloom's Taxonomy

Our resource is an effective tool for any ***GEOGRAPHY PROGRAM.***

Bloom's Taxonomy* for Reading Comprehension

The activities in this resource engage and build the full range of thinking skills that are essential for students' reading comprehension. Based on the six levels of thinking in Bloom's Taxonomy, assignments are given that challenge students to not only recall what they have read, but move beyond this to understand the text through higher-order thinking. By using higher-order skills of applying, analysing, evaluating and creating, students become active readers, drawing more meaning from the text, and applying and extending their learning in more sophisticated ways.

Our resource, therefore, is an effective tool for any Geography program. Whether it is used in whole or in part, or adapted to meet individual student needs, this resource provides teachers with the important questions to ask, interesting content, which promote creative and meaningful learning.

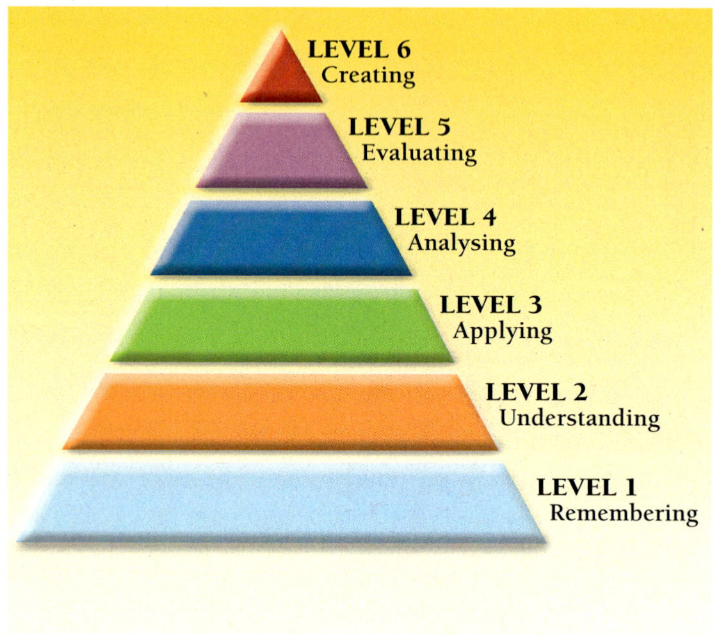

BLOOM'S TAXONOMY: 6 LEVELS OF THINKING

**Bloom's Taxonomy is a widely used tool by educators for classifying learning objectives, and is based on the work of Benjamin Bloom.*

Vocabulary

agriculture
amenities
author
axis
boundaries
capital city
cardinal directions
choropleth
climate
commercial
community
compass
compass rose
continents
contour lines
coordinates
country
culturally
date
direction
diverse
elevation
Equator
geographically
gradual
grid system
incline
index
industrialized
intermediate directions
landscape
latitude
legend
longitude
orientation
overseas
political maps
population
Prime Meridian
provinces
relation
residential
rural
scale
sea level
states
steep
surrounding area
symbols
territories
title
topographic
urban

NAME: ______________________

Basics of Map Reading

1. Match the word on the left to its definition on the right by drawing a line.

	Word	Definition	
1	compass	The name of the map	A
2	compass rose	The person who drew the map	B
3	legend	An instrument that shows the direction of travel	C
4	symbol	A symbol that shows direction	D
5	title	The places near the map	E
6	scale	The way the map is drawn on paper	F
7	author	A tool that shows what the distance on the map equals to on the ground	G
8	orientation	The main directions (North, South, East, West)	H
9	surrounding area	An explanation of the symbols used on the map	I
10	cardinal directions	Drawings that represent real things on land	J

NAME: 

Basics of Map Reading

Mapping Hint:

TODALSIGS =

Title, Orientation, Date, Author, Legend, Scale, Index, Grid System and Surrounding Areas.

The mnemonic TODALSIGS tells you everything you need to place on a map. It stands for Title, Orientation, Date, Author, Legend, Scale, Index, Grid System, and Surrounding Area.

All maps have **titles**, which tell us about the map. **Orientation** tells us how the map is drawn on the paper. Most maps have North at the top. The **date** and **author** tell us who wrote the map and when. The date can be important because maps and places change over time. The **legend** and **index** explain the symbols on the maps. Things such as schools, roads and railway tracks all have their own **symbols**. The **grid system** is a system of horizontal and vertical lines drawn on the map. The letters stand for columns and the numbers stand for rows. In this way, people can describe where things are located. For example, if you read in the index in the image below that there is a bridge at B5, you can find that bridge easily on your map. The final 'S' stands for **surrounding areas**. All maps show the places close to them. This helps people to understand where the map is in **relation** to other places. Relation means the location of a place or object when compared to another place or object. Also, people often use maps to go from one place to another place that is close by.

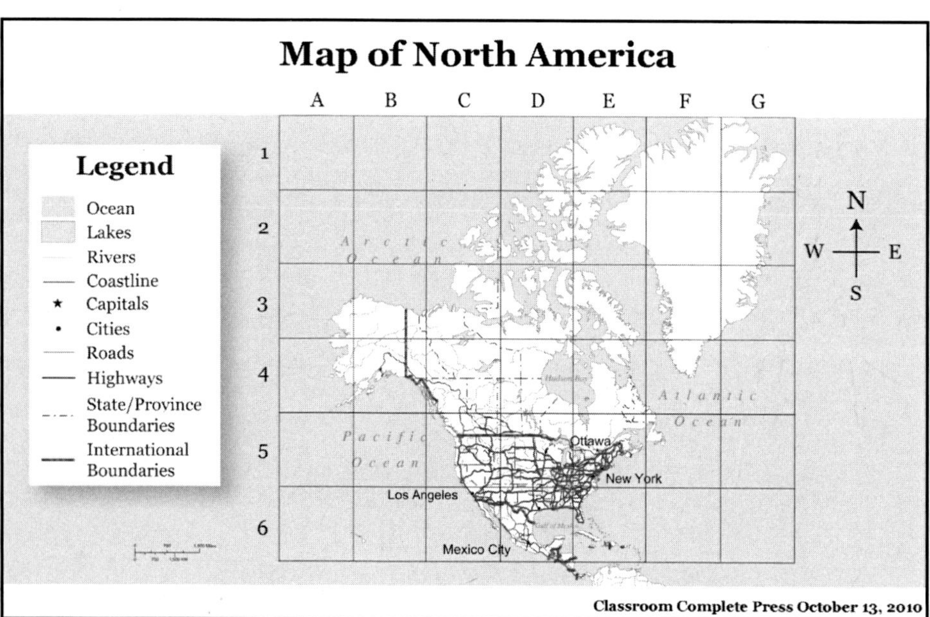

NAME: ______________________

Basics of Map Reading

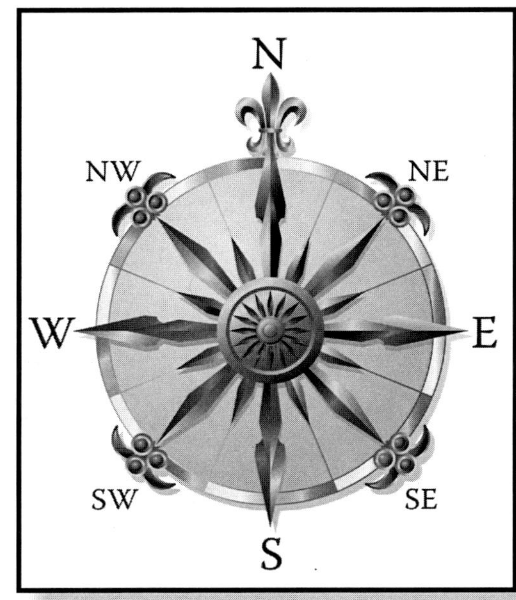

Direction

A **compass** is an instrument that shows which direction you are facing. A **compass rose** is a drawing that shows arrows pointing in several directions. It shows you where the *cardinal directions* are (North, South, East and West). It also shows you where the **intermediate directions** are (North East, South East, North West and South West).

Scale

The **scale** on a map shows you how much distance on the map equals how much distance on the Earth. For example, a scale of 1 inch = 1 mile or 1 cm = 1 km means that 1 inch or 1 centimeter on the map equals 1 mile or 1 kilometer on the Earth. Therefore, if something is 2 inches or 2 cm away on the map, it is actually 2 miles or 2 km away in real life. People use scales on a map to calculate the **distance** between two places.

To measure the actual distance between two places, you have to use a ruler and a scale. However, this method will only give you a straight-line distance between two points. If you wish, for example, to find the distance traveled by road between two points, you have to use string to trace the route. Then, place the string along the scale and measure.

Mapping Hint:

Straight line distances are also known as, 'as the crow flies.'

Explore with Google Earth™

Type in your hometown in the search field. Click on "View" in the top navigation bar and scroll down to "Scale Legend." Measure the length of the line. What is it? What is the number in the middle of the line? Try zooming in and out. What happens to the scale?

After You Read

NAME: ______________________

Basics of Map Reading

1. Fill in each blank with a word from the reading passage.

All maps have ________ (**a**), which tell us about the map. ____________ (**b**) tells us how the map is drawn on the paper. Most maps have _________ (**c**) at the top. The date and author tell us _______ (**d**) wrote the map and _________ (**e**). The _________ (**f**) and index explain the symbols on the maps. The ___________ (**g**) is a system of horizontal and ___________ (**h**) lines drawn on the map. The final 'S' stands for _________________ (**i**). All maps show the places close to them. This helps people to understand where the map is in ___________ (**j**) to other places.

2. Calculate the scale for the following scenarios.

a) If the scale is 1 cm (1 inch) on the map = 1 km (1 mile) on the ground, what would 5 cm (5 inches) on the map equal on the ground? ________________

b) If the scale is 1 inch (1 cm) on the map = 2 miles (2 km) on the ground, what would 10 inches (10 cm) on the map equal on the ground? ______________

c) If the scale is 1 cm (1 inch) on the map = 10 km (10 miles) on the ground, what would 10 cm (10 inches) on the map equal on the ground? _____________

d) If the scale is 1 inch (1 cm) on the map = 5 miles (5 km) on the ground, what would 15 inches (15 cm) on the map equal on the ground? ______________

e) If the scale is 1 inch (1 cm) on the map = 100 miles (100 km) on the ground, what would 8 inches (8 cm) on the map equal on the ground? ____________

NAME: ______________________________

Basics of Map Reading

Answer each question with a complete sentence.

3. What does the mnemonic TODALSIGS stand for?

____

4. What does orientation tell us?

____

5. What direction usually faces the top of the page? ______________

6. What do the legend and symbols on maps tell us?

____

7. Explain why using string to measure distance on a map could be more effective than using a ruler.

____

8. If a map has a scale of 1 inch = 1 mile, how many miles will 10 inches equal?

____

9. If a map has a scale of 2 cm = 1 km, how many km will 10 cm equal?

____

Research

10. Research both large and small-scale maps and practice finding the distances between places.

____

Map Activity

NAME: ____________________

Basics of Map Reading

Using the scale on the map, calculate (to the nearest mile/kilometer) how far the following objects are from each other. You may want to use a ruler or string to be accurate.

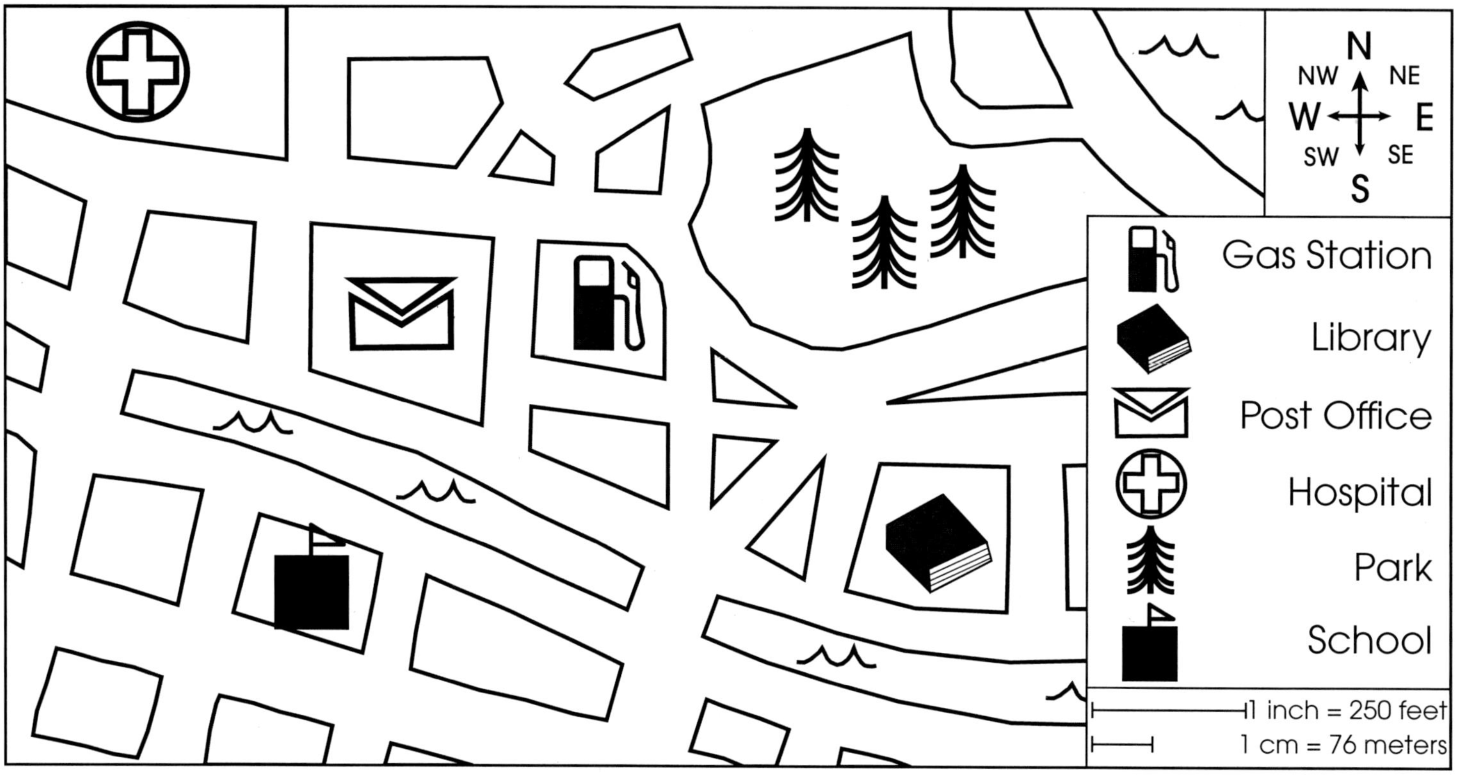

N NW NE W E SW SE S

Gas Station
Library
Post Office
Hospital
Park
School

1 inch = 250 feet
1 cm = 76 meters

1. From the library to the school. ____________________

2. From the gas station to the school. ____________________

3. From the hospital to the park. ____________________

4. From the park to the school. ____________________

5. From the park to the library. ____________________

6. From the post office to the park. ____________________

7. From the post office to the hospital. ____________________

8. From the gas station to the library. ____________________

NAME: ______________________________

Latitude, Longitude and Time Zones

1. Find the locations of the following objects by using the grid system below.

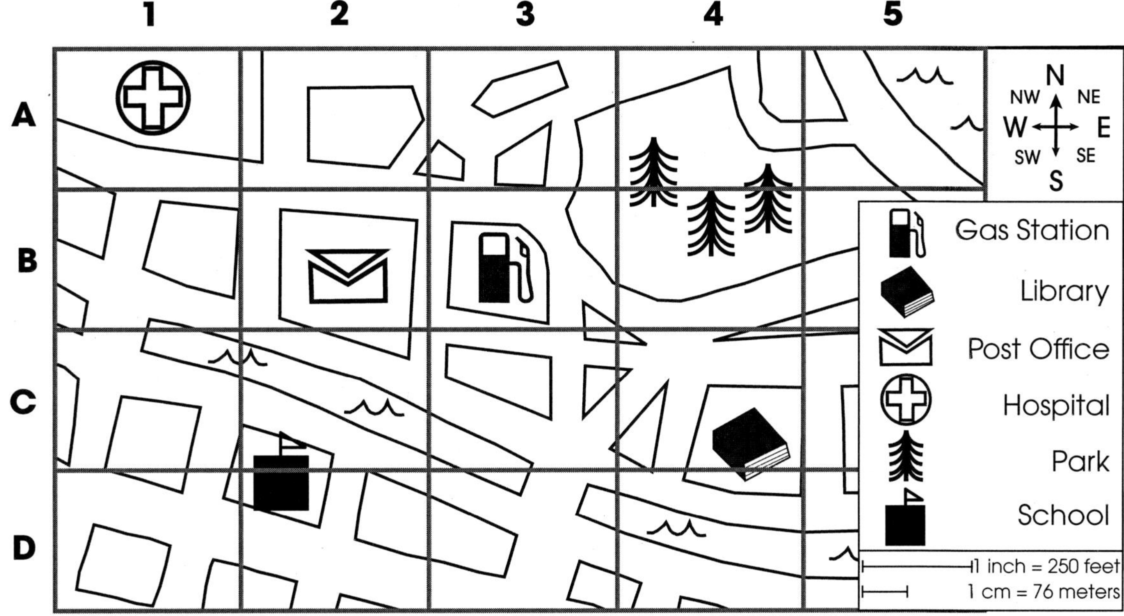

a) What object is located at B4? ______________________________

b) What object is located at A1? ______________________________

c) What object is located at C4? ______________________________

d) What object is located at B2? ______________________________

2. Circle the word **TRUE** if the statement is TRUE or **circle** the word **FALSE** if it is FALSE.

a) Longitude and latitude lines are imaginary.

TRUE **FALSE**

b) Longitude lines run from East to West.

TRUE **FALSE**

c) Latitude lines move from East to West.

TRUE **FALSE**

d) The Equator is an important line of latitude.

TRUE **FALSE**

NAME: ______________________

Latitude, Longitude and Time Zones

In order that people, could accurately explain, where things were in the world, it was necessary to agree upon the location of an imaginary grid. After much debate, it was agreed that the **Prime Meridian**, 0 degrees longitude, would be at Greenwich, England.

From that point, the Earth is divided by 360 degrees, which make a full circle of imaginary lines. The Earth is divided North to South by 180 degrees. The **Equator**, 0 degrees latitude, runs around the middle of the Earth, and there are 90 degrees North and 90 degrees South.

North Pole
Prime Meridian
Equator
South Pole

By giving **longitude** and **latitude coordinates**, it is possible to state where anything is located on the surface of the Earth.

Time Zones

The Earth rotates around the Sun and spins on its **axis** so different parts of the Earth face the Sun at different times. Everyone agreed that when the Sun is straight up in the sky, it is noon. Different parts of the Earth have the Sun straight up in the sky at different times. The Earth is a circle with 360 degrees. These degrees were divided by 24 (one hour for the 24 hours in a day). 360 degrees divided by 24 equals 15 degrees, which equals one hour. So, when it is noon at 0 degrees it is 1:00 pm at 15 degrees East and 2:00 pm at 30 degrees East.

Mapping Hint:

Remember longitude lines run long ways, from top to bottom, and latitude lines run from side to side, or East to West.

Explore with Google Earth™

Type your hometown into the search field. Click on "View" and "Toolbar" in the top navigation bar. Click the Sun image in the toolbar at the top of your screen and move the scale back and forth. What do you notice about the Sun's movement across the surface of the Earth as you adjust the time of day?

NAME: ______________________________

Latitude, Longitude and Time Zones

1. Circle the word **TRUE** if the statement is TRUE or circle the word **FALSE** if it is FALSE.

a) A grid is a way to locate places on a map.

TRUE **FALSE**

b) A grid is a series of squiggly lines, which explain height or elevation.

TRUE **FALSE**

c) Latitude and longitude lines make a type of grid.

TRUE **FALSE**

d) The Equator is located at 0 degrees longitude.

TRUE **FALSE**

e) The Prime Meridian is an important line of longitude.

TRUE **FALSE**

f) The Equator is located at 0 degrees latitude.

TRUE **FALSE**

g) The Earth rotates around the Sun and on its axis.

TRUE **FALSE**

h) Time zones give the time at different regions of the Earth.

TRUE **FALSE**

i) Longitude lines run from East to West.

TRUE **FALSE**

j) Lines of latitude run from top to bottom.

TRUE **FALSE**

After You Read

NAME: ______________________

Latitude, Longitude and Time Zones

Answer each question with a complete sentence.

2. Imagine you are an immigrant to the United States and you want to explain to someone how to get from New York City to your hometown. Tell them how to get there.

____

____

____

____

____

3. Why would it be easier to use longitude and latitude to explain where you are?

____

____

4. How do grids help you find places on a map?

____

____

Research

5. Use an atlas, to find the longitude and latitude coordinates of 10 major North American cities.

City	Coordinates

NAME: ______________________

Map Activity

Latitude, Longitude and Time Zones

Look at the map of the United States. In 1850, John and his family left New York, to look for gold in California. Answer the following questions by using the map. Remember: each line of longitude equals 15 degrees, which equals one hour.

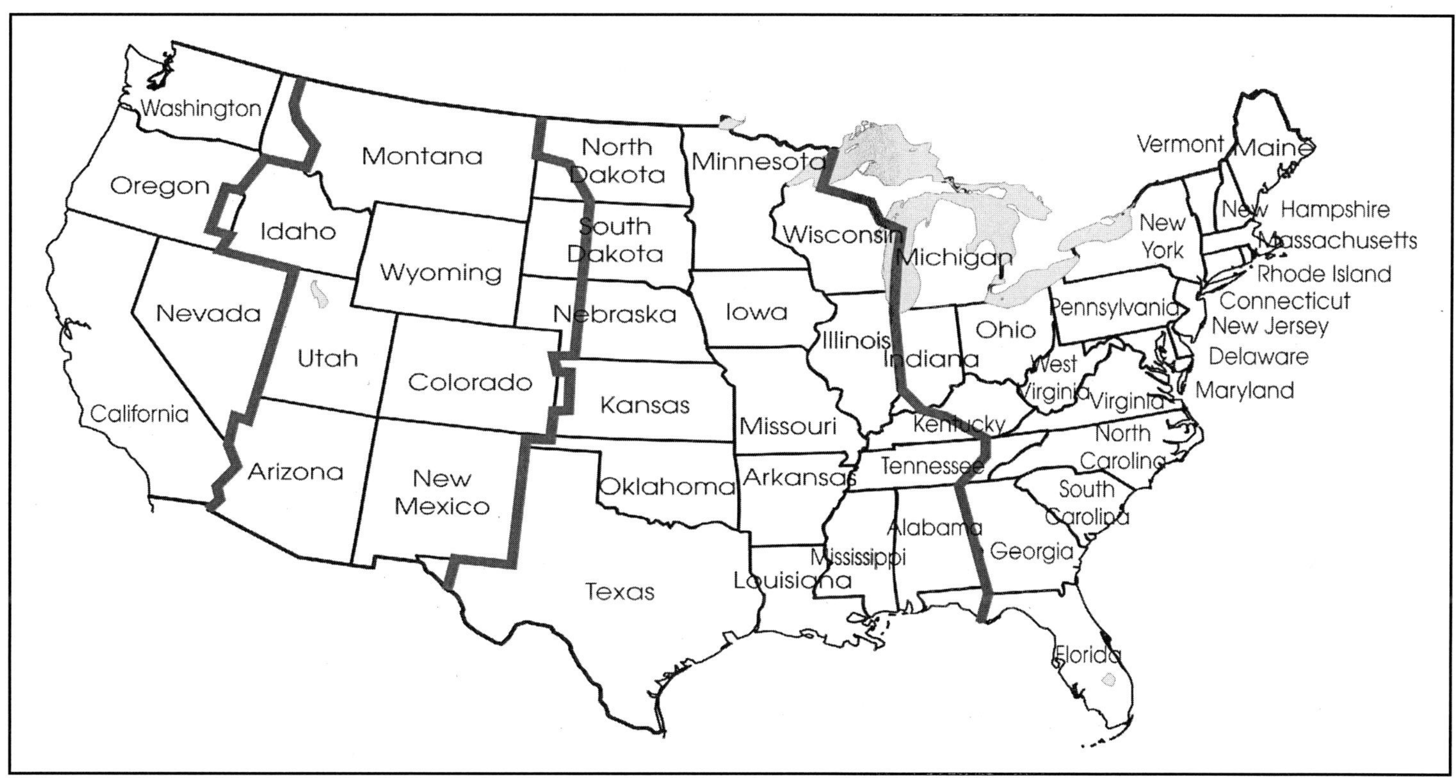

1. If it is noon in New York, what time is it in Colorado? ______________________

2. If it is noon in New York, what time is it in California? ______________________

3. If it is noon in New York, what time is it in Nebraska? ______________________

4. If it is noon in New York, what time is it in Florida? ______________________

5. What is the time difference between the East and West coast? ______________________

6. If you travel West, does the time decrease or increase? ______________________

NAME: ______________________

Mapping Geographical Features

1. Put a check mark (✓) next to the answer that is most correct.

a) What is a desert?

- ○ **A** A dry, often sandy region of little rainfall and little vegetation.
- ○ **B** A region of permanent cold that is largely absent of life.
- ○ **C** An area covered with trees.
- ○ **D** All of the above.

b) What is a mountain?

- ○ **A** A natural elevation of the Earth's surface with generally steep sides, and taller than a hill.
- ○ **B** A natural elevation over 984 feet/300 meters tall.
- ○ **C** A natural elevation shorter than a hill.
- ○ **D** Both A and B.

c) What is a valley?

- ○ **A** A lowland between ranges of mountains or hills.
- ○ **B** A barren area.
- ○ **C** A dry sandy region.
- ○ **D** None of the above.

d) What is a lake?

- ○ **A** A large body of water, that is separated by continents.
- ○ **B** An inland body of fresh water surrounded by land.
- ○ **C** An inland body of salt water surrounded by land.
- ○ **D** Both B and C.

e) What is sea level?

- ○ **A** The distance you can see.
- ○ **B** The height of the sea at low tide.
- ○ **C** The height of the sea at high tide.
- ○ **D** The height that is the halfway point between high and low tides.

NAME: ______________________

Mapping Geographical Features

All maps have their own way of communicating meaning. **Political maps** show **boundaries** between states or provinces. The states and provinces are usually written in capital letters. Capitals of states, provinces and territories usually have a square to mark their location. Maps use colors, which represent the things on the ground. For example, bodies of water, such as rivers, lakes and oceans, are usually colored blue. Forests and other plant areas are colored green. Buildings and roads are colored black. Brown is used to show deserts, historical buildings and national parks.

A topographic map showing steep elevation

Topographic maps show differences in **elevation** or height. They are either black or brown in color. The lines, or **contour lines**, connect points of land that are the same height. When the lines are close together, the land is **steep**. When the topographic lines are far apart, the area has a **gradual incline**. Elevation begins at **sea level**, which is the height of the sea in between high and low tides.

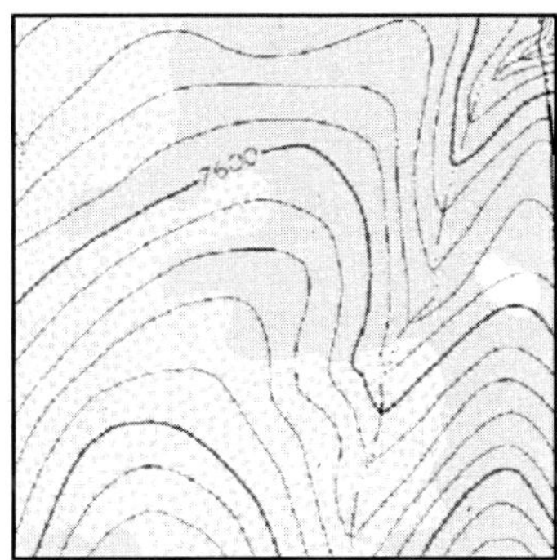

A topographic map showing gradual elevation

Mapping Hint:

Colors on maps, which are used to represent things on land, usually resemble the things they represent.

Explore with Google Earth™

Type in your hometown into the search field. Click on "View" and "Status Bar" in the top navigation bar. At the bottom of the screen you will see a set of numbers. They show the coordinates of your hometown, then the elevation. What do you notice about the elevation numbers as you move your mouse from the green to brown areas?

After You Read

NAME: ____________________

Mapping Geographical Features

1. Match the word on the left to its definition on the right by drawing a line.

	Word	Definition	
1	topographic map	A map, which shows the boundaries of cities, states, provinces and countries	A
2	elevation	A rapid rise in elevation	B
3	contour line	A slow rise in elevation	C
4	steep	A map, which shows geographical features such as forests and hills	D
5	gradual	The height that is exactly half way between low and high tide	E
6	political map	A line on a map, which connects points of land that are the same height	F
7	sea level	A change in height	G
8	green	The color that represents forests and vegetation	H
9	brown	The color that represents deserts and national parks	I

NAME: ______________________________

Mapping Geographical Features

Answer each question with a complete sentence.

2. In which instances would topographical maps be better than political maps?

____

____

3. In which cases would political maps be better than topographic maps?

____

____

4. If you were hiking and the topographic map you had, showed a lot of brown squiggly lines very close together, what would you expect?

____

____

5. If you were traveling to Florida, what type of map would you use?

____

____

6. If your map had a lot of blue on it, what would you expect?

____

____

7. Imagine you have been lost in the woods. On your map, you see you are approaching a black line. Would you be happy? Why?

____

____

____

Research

8. Investigate local topographical maps and list all of the things you can find in a small area. Look at a state/provincial map of the same area and list what it shows for that area.

Map Activity

NAME: ______________________________

Mapping Geographical Features

Draw a map of a country, using appropriate symbols and a legend. Your country should include a mountain, a forest, a desert area and at least one body of water.

LEGEND

NAME: ______________________________

Mapping Cultural Features

1. Draw an urban community. Label as many things as possible.

2. Draw a rural community. Label as many things as possible.

3. Match the word on the left to its definition on the right by drawing a line.

	Word	Definition	
1	urban	Relating to the countryside	A
2	rural	Built up areas such as cities or towns	B
3	community	Comforts and convenient features	C
4	amenity	A group with shared characteristics	D

NAME: ______________________

Mapping Cultural Features

What is a community?

A **community** is a group of people who share common interests, characteristics and experiences. People from the same community live in the same area. Communities should be friendly, safe and clean. Unfortunately, this is not true of all communities in the world.

Urban Community

Rural Community

Urban communities have a lot of people in an area. **Rural** communities have fewer people and they are more spread out. Urban communities have schools, hospitals, libraries and other **amenities**. Rural communities are set in the countryside outside of cities and tend to have fewer amenities. Rural communities used to be dominated by farming. However, now many people move to the countryside because they are able to work from home and they want a quieter life. Mining and forestry used to employ a lot of people who lived in rural communities. Fewer people are now needed in these jobs due to the advancements made in technology. Many people live in cities because it is close to where they work. Because there are more businesses and people in cities, there are naturally more jobs in urban areas.

Mapping Hint:

In urban communities, most of the land is used for **residential** or **commercial** purposes. In rural communities, most of the land is used for **agriculture** or parks.

Most urban or rural communities are developed where they are because of the environment. For example, many urban centers are on great lakes or rivers, because this provided drinking water and a transportation route. Many rural communities are where they are because the land was good for farming.

Look at a major city such as Toronto or New York. Look at a rural area in Nebraska or Saskatchewan. What differences do you see?

NAME: ____________________

Mapping Cultural Features

1. From these photos, what can you say about a community that is urban?

____

____

____

____

2. Make a list of 3 things that you can do in both the city and the countryside.

- ______________________________
- ______________________________
- ______________________________

3. List the 3 advantages of living in an urban community and the advantages of living in a rural community.

- ______________________________
- ______________________________
- ______________________________

4. Circle the word **TRUE** if the statement is TRUE or circle the word **FALSE** if it is FALSE.

a) A community is a group of people who share common interests, characteristics and experiences.

TRUE **FALSE**

b) People from the same community do not live in the same area.

TRUE **FALSE**

c) All communities are friendly, safe and clean.

TRUE **FALSE**

After You Read

NAME: ______________________

Mapping Cultural Features

Answer each question with a complete sentence.

5. What is a community?

____

____

6. What makes a good community?

____

____

7. What's the difference between a rural and urban community?

____

____

____

8. Why do people live in your community?

____

____

9. List 3 reasons to visit rural communities.

____

____

____

10. List 3 reasons to visit urban communities.

____

____

____

Research

11. If you could live anywhere in the world, where would you choose? Why would you choose this place? Research your chosen place and write a one-page paper explaining your choice.

NAME: ______________________________

Map Activity

Mapping Cultural Features

Draw a map of a rural area. Draw a map of an urban area. Draw a 10 x 10 grid over top of both maps. Each square equals 1%. Make a chart, which shows (roughly) how land is used. Categories you may wish to consider are: farming, parks and recreation, residential, industrial, transportation and government buildings.

NAME: ____________________

Map Your Country

Answer each question with a complete sentence.

1. Which continent are the United States and Canada part of?

____

2. What is the name of the ocean on the East coast of the United States and Canada?

____

3. What is the name of the ocean on the West coast of the United States and Canada?

____

4. What type of map shows cities, states/provinces and national boundaries?

____

5. List as many states and provinces that you can.

1. ______	21. ______	41. ______
2. ______	22. ______	42. ______
3. ______	23. ______	43. ______
4. ______	24. ______	44. ______
5. ______	25. ______	45. ______
6. ______	26. ______	46. ______
7. ______	27. ______	47. ______
8. ______	28. ______	48. ______
9. ______	29. ______	49. ______
10. ______	30. ______	50. ______
11. ______	31. ______	51. ______
12. ______	32. ______	52. ______
13. ______	33. ______	53. ______
14. ______	34. ______	54. ______
15. ______	35. ______	55. ______
16. ______	36. ______	56. ______
17. ______	37. ______	57. ______
18. ______	38. ______	58. ______
19. ______	39. ______	59. ______
20. ______	40. ______	60. ______

NAME: ______________________

Map Your Country

The United States and Canada are both massive countries. They have large urban centers and rural areas, which are dominated by farming and agriculture. Some areas of the **country**, such as the Great Plains in the United States and the Prairies in Canada are flat. While other areas, such as the Appalachian Mountains and the Rocky Mountains have large elevations. There are many different types of maps, which give us information about our country. **Political maps** show towns, cities, counties, states and provinces and international boundaries. **Topographic maps** show natural things such as rivers and elevation. Topographic maps tend to be more detailed than political maps.

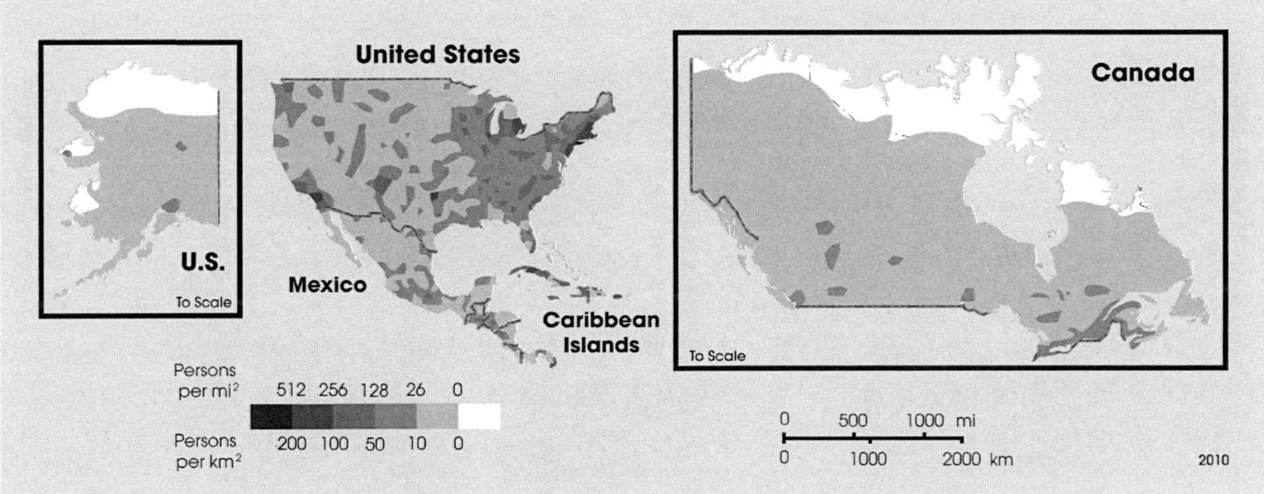

A choropleth map showing the population density for North America.

A third type of map is a **choropleth map**. These maps give us information about places. Choropleth maps can be used to compare different regions and compare information, known as data. For example, choropleth maps can be used to express information about **population**. They use color as a code that explains information. Choropleth maps are also used to give information about the weather. They have many different colors and can be used to teach people about rainfall or temperature in different areas.

Mapping Hint:

Because of the different climates and geography, people do different things in these areas. They have different hobbies, different jobs and grow different foods.

NAME: ________________________________

Map Your Country

Each country has a **capital city**. In the United States for example, the capital is Washington D.C. All **states, territories** and **provinces** also have capital cities. The United States has 50 states, while Canada has 10 provinces and 3 very large areas known as territories. The **climate** and **landscape** vary greatly across both of these countries. Parts of Canada are very cold, nearly all year round, while parts of the United States are very warm, even in the winter.

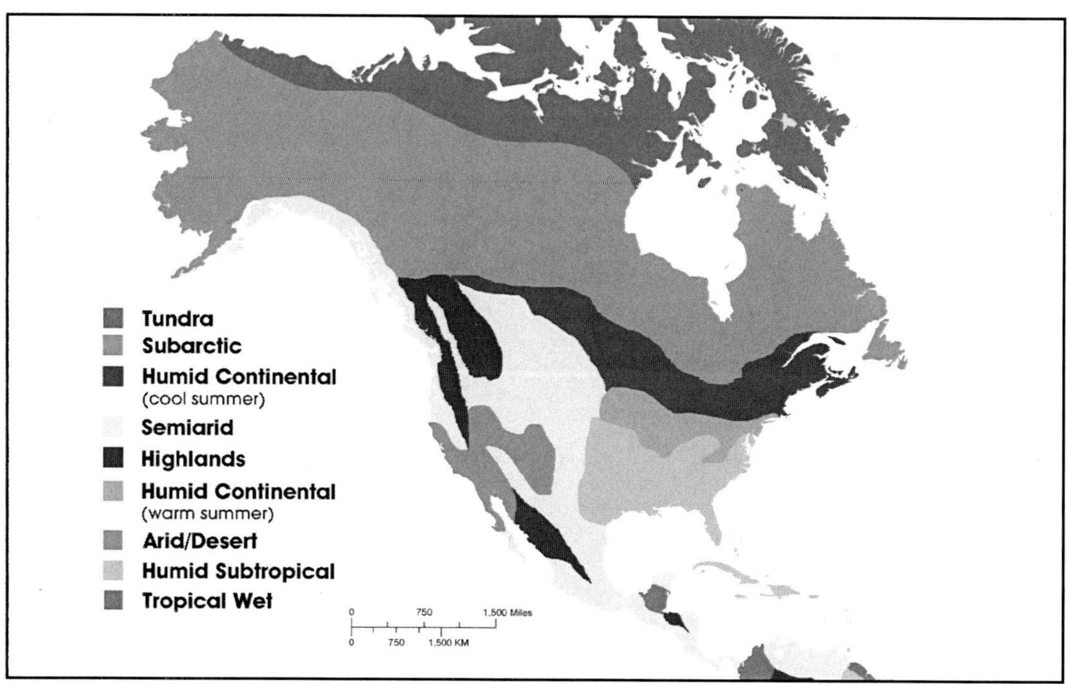

A choropleth map showing the climate regions of North America. See Choropleth Map overhead on page 56 for the climate regions of the world.

Explore with Google Earth™

Type in your hometown into the search field. In the layers panel in the side navigation tab, click "Weather." What do you notice about the weather in your area?

NAME: ______________________________

Map Your Country

1. Fill in each blank with a word from the reading passage.

The United States and Canada are both massive ____________(a). They have large urban centers and ____________(b) areas, which are dominated by farming and agriculture. Some areas of the country, such as the Great Plains in the United States and the Prairies in Canada are ____________(c). While other areas, such as the Appalachian Mountains and the ____________(d) Mountains have large elevations. ____________(e) maps show towns, cities, counties, states and provinces and international boundaries. ____________(f) maps show natural things such as rivers and elevation.

2. Circle the word **TRUE** if the statement is TRUE or circle the word **FALSE** if it is FALSE.

a) The capital city of the United States is Washington D.C.

TRUE **FALSE**

b) All states, territories and provinces also have capital cities.

TRUE **FALSE**

c) The United States has 53 states.

TRUE **FALSE**

d) Canada has 10 provinces and 3 very large areas known as territories.

TRUE **FALSE**

After You Read

NAME: ______________________

Map Your Country

Answer each question with a complete sentence.

3. What is the name of your home state/province?

____

4. What is the capital city of that state/province?

____

5. What is the capital city of your country?

____

6. What is the ocean to the East of your country?

____

7. What is the ocean to the West of your country?

____

8. What is a political map?

____

____

9. What is a topographical map?

____

____

10. What is a choropleth map?

____

____

Research

11. Research and list as many states/provinces/territories and their capital cities as you can, on a separate piece of paper.

NAME: ______________________________

Map Your Country

1. Draw a map of your country. Label your state/province and any other states/provinces/ territories that you know.
2. Draw and label the great lakes, the oceans and at least one major river. Color them blue.
3. Draw a mountain range.
4. Give your map a title, compass rose, date, author, legend, and a grid.
5. What are the coordinates of your home state/province?
6. Label the surrounding countries.

NAME: ____________________

Map the World

1. Put a check mark (✓) next to the answer that is most correct.

a) What is a continent?

- ◯ **A** A massive body of salt water, which covers 70% of the Earth.
- ◯ **B** One of the main land masses of the Earth usually regarded as including Africa, Antarctica, Asia, Australia, Europe, North America, and South America.
- ◯ **C** A large tract of land, which is recognizable by its land or culture.

b) What is an ocean?

- ◯ **A** A massive body of salt water, which covers 70% of the Earth.
- ◯ **B** One of the main land masses of the Earth usually regarded as including Africa, Antarctica, Asia, Australia, Europe, North America, and South America.
- ◯ **C** A large tract of land, which is recognizable by its land or culture.

c) What is a country?

- ◯ **A** A massive body of salt water, which covers 70% of the Earth.
- ◯ **B** One of the main land masses of the Earth usually regarded as including Africa, Antarctica, Asia, Australia, Europe, North America, and South America.
- ◯ **C** A large tract of land, which is recognizable by its land or culture.

d) What is the world?

- ◯ **A** The continents, the oceans and all the natural things, and human-made features, which occur on our planet.
- ◯ **B** The fourth planet from the Sun.
- ◯ **C** The countries and lakes.

e) How much of the Earth's surface is covered by water?

- ◯ **A** 90%
- ◯ **B** 50%
- ◯ **C** 70%

NAME: ______________________________

Map the World

The world contains seven **continents**, which are massive areas of land. Most people think the world also contains four oceans and numerous seas. However, some scientists consider the area around Antarctica to be the 5th ocean, which is known as the Southern Ocean. Seventy percent of the Earth's surface is covered by water. The seven continents are in order of size: Asia, Africa, North America, South America, Antarctica, Europe and Australia.

A **country** is a unique area of land defined **geographically, culturally** or both. The world contains 195 countries at this time. The number of countries in the world changes constantly, as people occasionally decide they are different in culture and geography to those within their **boundaries**.

North America is the third largest continent. The United States and Canada are some of the richest countries in the world. They are very **industrialized** and sell a lot of products

NAME: ______________________________

Map the World

overseas. Canada is very fortunate because it has a lot of natural products, such as wood and gas, which it can sell overseas. Haiti, on the other hand is one of the poorest countries in the world. Many of the countries in the Caribbean rely on tourism to make money. One of the reasons they can do this is because they have very warm weather and lovely beaches. The weather gets warmer as one moves further south in North America.

Greenland and parts of Canada are beyond the Arctic Circle. It is very cold in this part of the world. Not many people live in this area because the weather is extremely cold and it is hard to grow food.

Mapping Hint:

The names of the continents can be easily remembered, if you think "6 A's and an E." Of course in this hint we think of North and South America as beginning with an A.

The world is a very **diverse** place and people live very differently in the many places of the world. For example, parts of Africa have very little clean drinking water, so they must be very careful to conserve water.

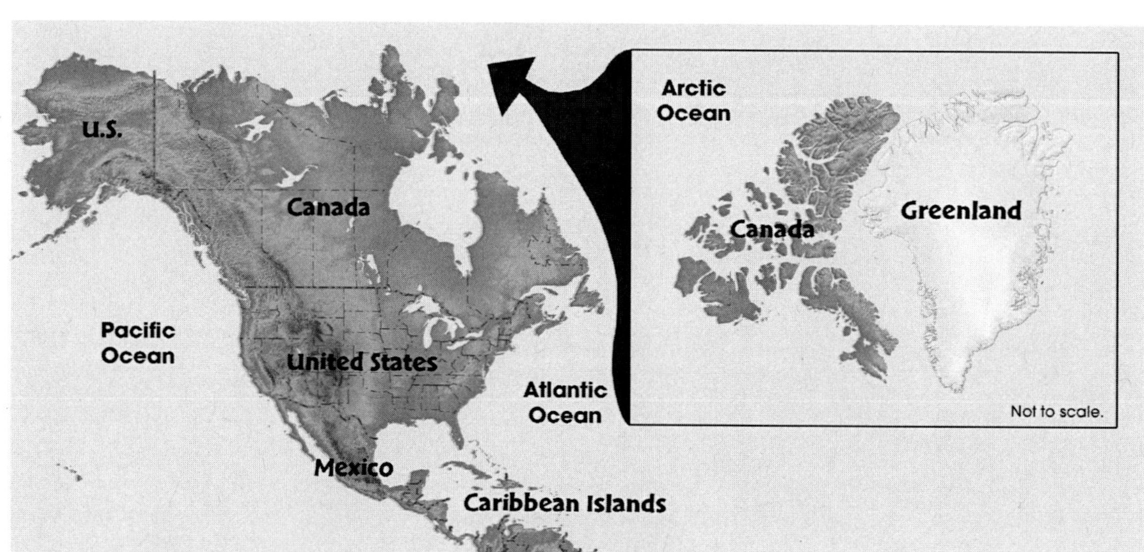

Explore with Google Earth™

Locate the 7 continents and 4 oceans. Type "Antarctica" into the search field and compare it with the other continents. Why would scientists consider the water around it to be its own ocean? Why do you think not many people live there?

NAME: ______________________

Map the World

1. Fill in each blank with a word from the reading passage.

The world contains seven continents, which are ______________ (a). Most people think the world also contains ______ (b) oceans and seven seas. However, some scientists consider the area around ____________ (c), to be the 5th ocean, which is known as the ____________ (d) Ocean. __________ (e) percent of the Earth's surface is covered by water. The seven continents are in order of size: Asia, ______ (f), North America, South America, __________ (g), Europe and __________ (h).

A country is a unique area of land defined geographically, ______________ (i) or both. The world contains _______ (j) countries at this time. The number of countries in the world __________ (k) constantly, as people occasionally decide they are different in culture and geography to those within their boundaries.

The world is a very _____________ (l) and people live very differently in the many places of the world. For example, parts of ___________ (m) have very little clean drinking water, so they must be very careful to ____________ (n) water.

After You Read

NAME: ____________________

Map the World

Answer each question with a complete sentence.

2. Name 3 countries in North America.

- ______________________
- ______________________
- ______________________

3. Name 4 countries in Africa.

- ______________________
- ______________________
- ______________________
- ______________________

4. Name 3 countries in each of the following continents: Europe, Asia and South America.

Continents	Countries	Countries	Countries
Europe			
Asia			
South America			

Research

5. Label the map of the world according to temperature. The classifications are A, tropical; B, dry; C, mild mid-latitude; D, cold mid-latitude; and E, polar. You will need to talk to your teacher or do further research to complete this activity.

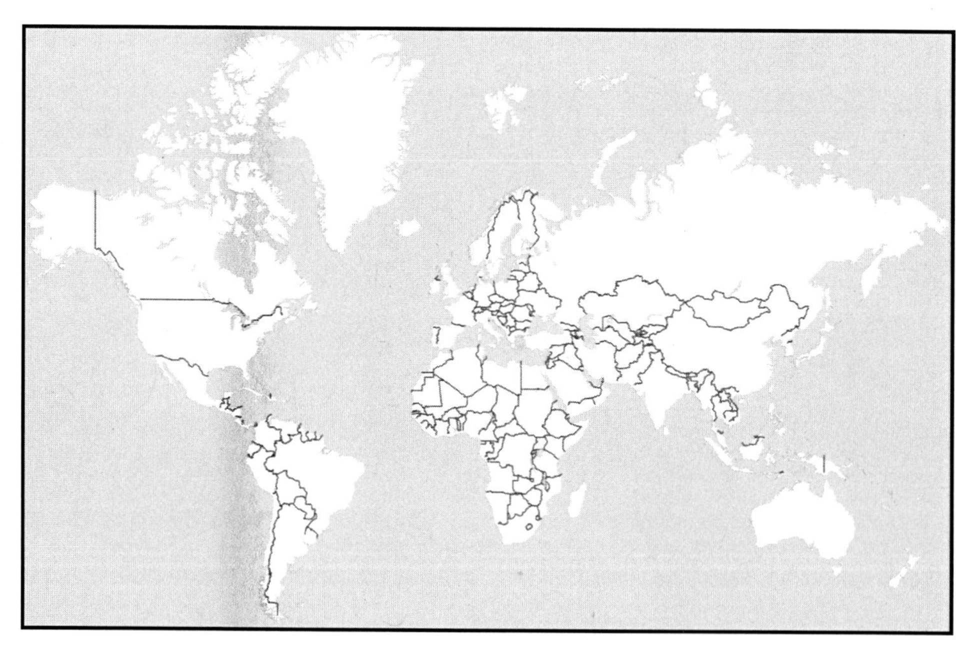

Map the World

Label the 7 continents and 4 oceans on the world map below. Label the United States, Canada, Mexico and Greenland.

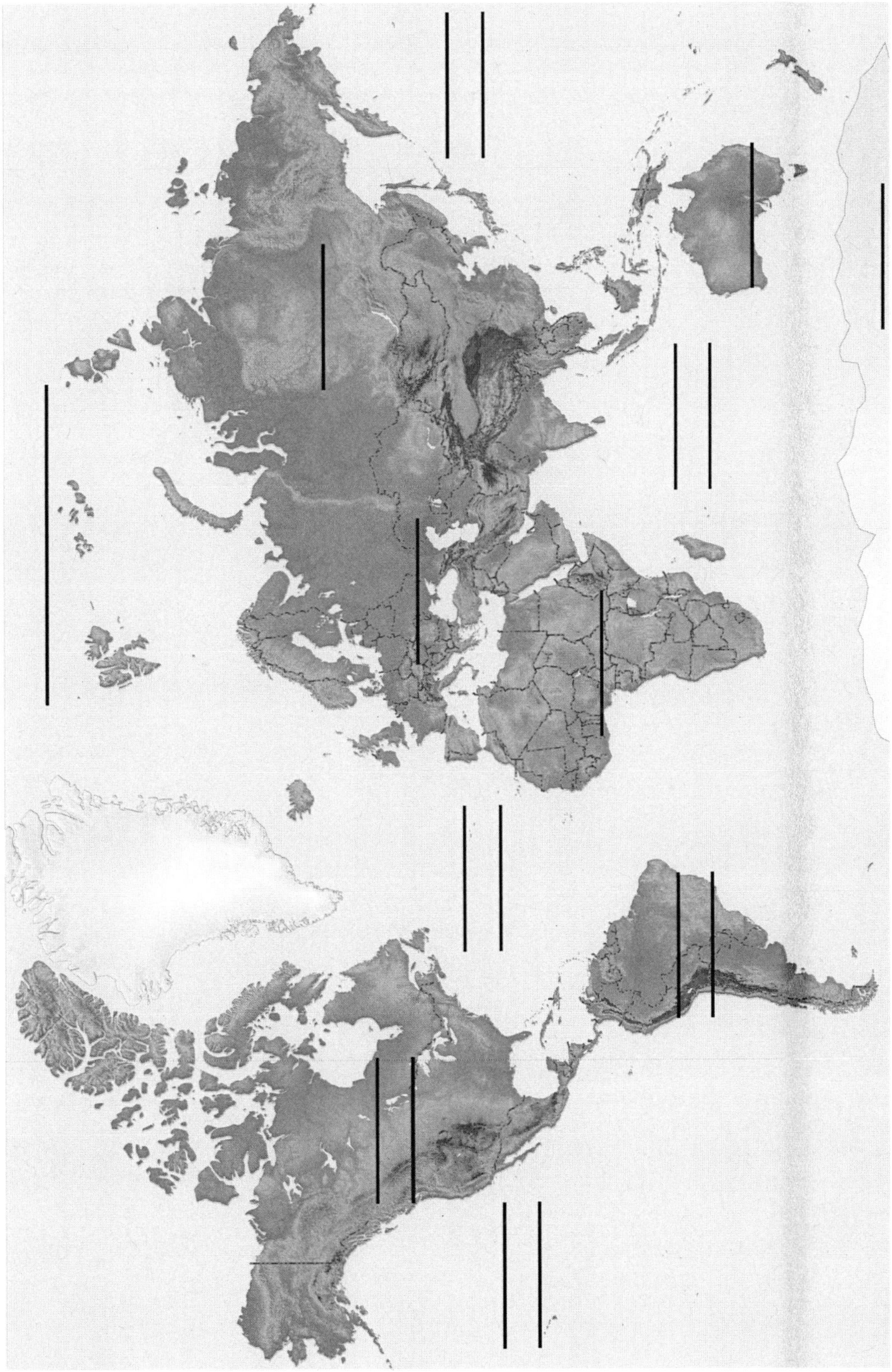

After You Read

NAME: ______________________

Crossword Puzzle!

Across

3. Maps that can be used to compare different regions and compare information, known as data.
4. If contour lines are close together on a map, it means the hill is ____________.
6. A tool that shows what the distance on the map equals on the ground.
8. 0 degrees longitude.
11. The person who wrote the map.
12. The name of the map.
13. The elevation half way between low and high tide.

Down

1. An imaginary line on the Earth, which travels horizontally around the globe.
2. A diagram on a map, which shows direction.
5. The main directions are called ______________ directions.
7. A group of people who share common interests, characteristics and experiences.
9. Urban communities have more of these than rural communities. They include hospitals and libraries.
10. The mnemonic that helps you remember, everything you need to place on a map.

1 2 3 4 5 6 7 8 9 10 11 12 13

Word List

amenities
author
cardinal
choropleth
community
compass rose
latitude
prime meridian
scale
sea level
steep
title
todalsigs

NAME: ______________________________

Word Search

Find all the words in the Word Search. Words are written horizontally, vertically, diagonally, and some are written backwards.

amenity	community	cultural	prime meridian	state
author	compass rose	equator	province	steep
boundary	continent	gradual	rural	territory
capital	coordinates	legend	scale	topographic
cardinal directions	country	political	sea level	urban

c	o	m	p	a	s	s	r	o	s	e	l	e	g	e	n	d	m
s	l	o	o	u	r	b	a	n	e	r	y	t	l	n	u	m	m
e	s	c	e	t	e	r	r	i	t	o	r	y	i	o	p	o	l
r	s	a	o	h	n	a	i	d	i	r	e	m	e	m	i	r	p
t	t	d	o	u	h	v	e	b	c	n	r	t	n	s	s	s	b
c	a	r	d	i	n	a	l	d	i	r	e	c	t	i	o	n	s
d	t	c	l	d	r	t	e	f	e	y	r	a	d	n	u	o	b
e	e	o	u	c	f	e	r	g	r	g	s	t	k	t	r	r	t
p	q	o	r	i	q	u	i	y	c	o	n	t	i	n	e	n	t
u	u	r	y	h	e	e	r	p	o	l	i	t	i	c	a	l	l
e	a	d	t	p	c	s	a	w	l	o	y	t	i	n	e	m	a
c	t	i	i	a	u	s	e	r	l	c	a	p	i	t	a	l	u
n	o	n	n	r	l	t	a	a	h	v	k	j	y	u	u	e	d
i	r	a	u	g	t	o	r	u	l	h	l	l	p	j	l	d	a
v	u	t	m	o	u	u	d	t	n	e	o	m	s	e	k	e	r
o	l	e	m	p	r	v	e	h	l	o	v	e	o	m	e	r	g
r	o	s	o	o	a	q	h	o	a	d	r	e	n	s	j	t	d
p	j	l	c	t	l	r	u	r	t	v	d	e	l	a	c	s	s

After You Read

NAME: ______________________________

Comprehension Quiz

Part A

1. What is an instrument, which shows the direction of travel? 

   ____

2. What is a tool that shows what the distance on the map equals on the ground? ______________________________ 

3. If the scale is 1 inch on the map = 1 mile on the ground. What would 5 inches on the map equal on the ground? ______________ 

4. If the scale is 1 cm on the map = 100 km on the ground. What would 8 cm on the map equal on the ground? ______________ 

5. What does the mnemonic TODALSIGS stand for? 

   ____

6. If it is noon in New York, what time is it in Florida? ______________ 

Part B

1. The Equator is located at 0 degrees latitude. **TRUE/FALSE** 

2. Lines of latitude run from top to bottom. **TRUE/FALSE** 

3. On the map of the world, label the 7 continents, 4 oceans, Greenland, the United States, and Canada. 

SUBTOTAL: /30

NAME: ______________________

Comprehension Quiz

Part C

Answer each question in complete sentences.

1. **What are lines of latitude and longitude?** 2

____

2. **How do grids help you to locate places on a map?** 1

____

3. **What is the difference between a political map and a topographic map?** 2

____

4. **What is the difference between rural and urban communities?** 2

____

5. **Describe the world, including the following terms: continents, oceans, water, diverse, countries.** 5

____

SUBTOTAL: /12

EZ✓

1.

1 C

2 D

3 I

4 J

5 A

6 G

7 B

8 F

9 E

10 H

(7)

1.

a) titles

b) orientation

c) North

d) who

e) when

f) legend

g) grid system

h) vertical

i) surrounding area

j) relation

2.

a) 5 km (5 miles)

b) 20 miles (20 km)

c) 100 km (100 miles)

d) 75 miles (75 km)

e) 800 miles (800 km)

(10)

3.

TODALSIGS stands for title, orientation, date, author, legend, scale, index, grid system, surrounding areas.

4.

Orientation tells us how the map is drawn on the paper.

5.

North usually faces the top of the page.

6.

Symbols represent objects such as schools, roads and railway tracks. Legends explain the symbols on maps.

7.

A ruler will only give you a straight-line distance between two points. To find the distance traveled by road between two points, you have to use string.

8.

10 inches would equal 10 miles.

9.

10 cm would equal 5 km.

10.

Students should become familiar with scales and measuring distance.

(11)

Map Activity

Answers may vary slightly.

1. 750 feet, 532 meters
2. 1000 feet, 722 meters
3. 500 feet, 418 meters
4. 875 feet, 646 meters
5. 125 feet, 114 meters
6. 250 feet, 190 meters
7. 62.5 feet, 76 meters
8. 375 feet, 266 meters

(12)

1.

a) Park

b) Hospital

c) Library

d) Post Office

2.

a) TRUE

b) FALSE

c) TRUE

d) TRUE

(13)

1.

a) TRUE

b) FALSE

c) TRUE

d) FALSE

e) TRUE

f) TRUE

g) TRUE

h) TRUE

i) FALSE

j) FALSE

(15)

2.

Answers may vary.

3.

Answers may vary. Longitude and latitude allows you to narrow down to the exact location on Earth.

4.

Grids divide the Earth into equal sections that help narrow down locations.

5.

Answers may vary. Coordinates for the cities chosen should be accurate.

16

Map Activity

1. 10:00 am

2. 9:00 am

3. 11:00 am

4. noon

5. 3 hours

6. decrease

17

1.

a) A

b) D

c) A

d) D

e) D

18

1.

1 D

2 G

3 F

4 B

5 C

6 A

7 E

8 H

9 I

20

2.

Answers may vary. When you want detailed information about a small area.

3.

Answers may vary. When you want information about larger areas such as countries or states.

4.

Answers may vary. A hilly area.

5.

Answers may vary. A road map.

6.

Answers may vary. You were near a body of water.

7.

Answers may vary. Yes. A black line would indicate a road.

8.

Answers may vary.

21

Map Activity

Answers may vary. Each map should be of a country and should indicate a mountain, a forest, a desert area, one body of water, symbols, and a legend.

22

EZ✓

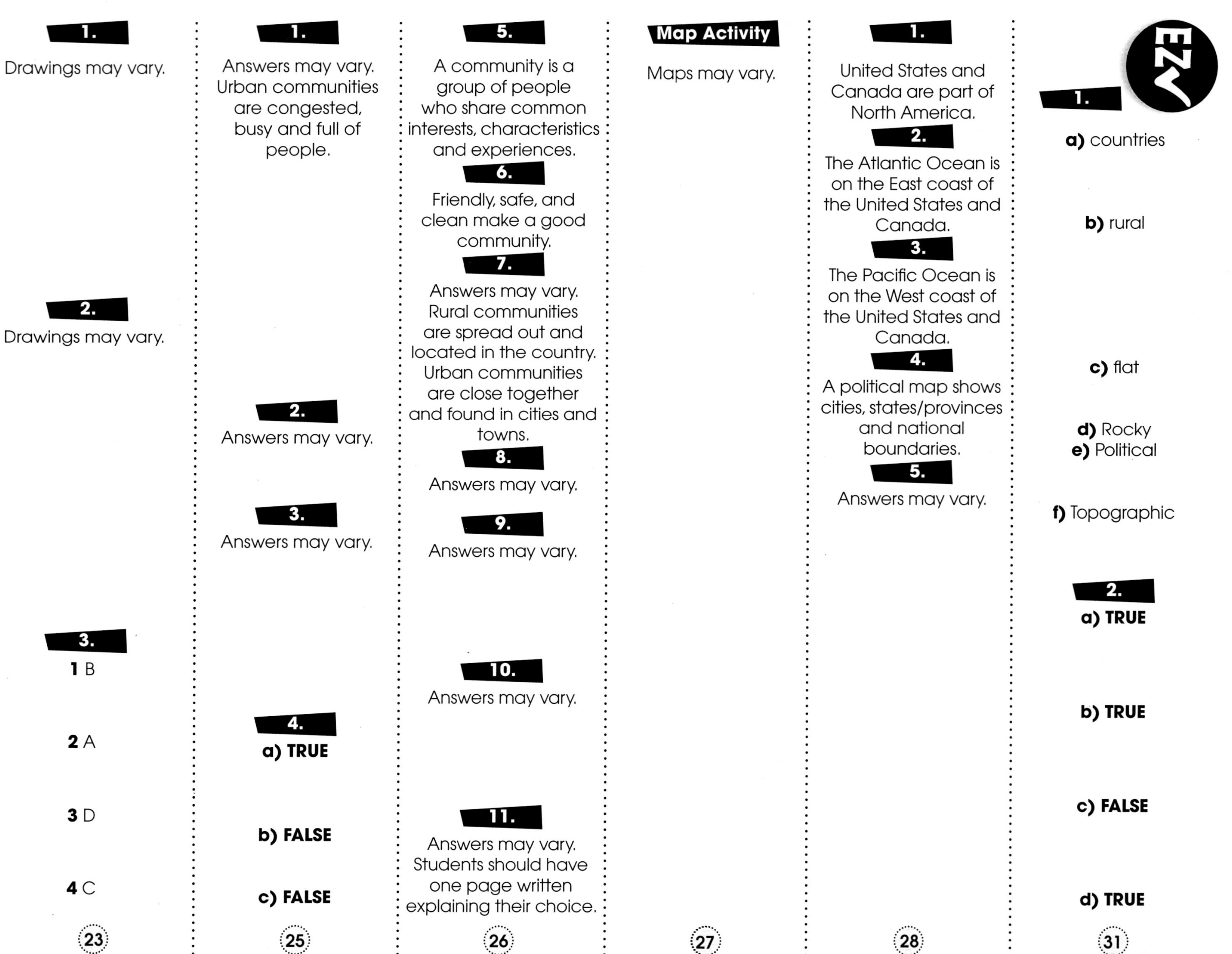

1. Drawings may vary.

2. Drawings may vary.

3.
1 B
2 A
3 D
4 C

(23)

1. Answers may vary. Urban communities are congested, busy and full of people.

2. Answers may vary.

3. Answers may vary.

4.
a) TRUE
b) FALSE
c) FALSE

(25)

5. A community is a group of people who share common interests, characteristics and experiences.

6. Friendly, safe, and clean make a good community.

7. Answers may vary. Rural communities are spread out and located in the country. Urban communities are close together and found in cities and towns.

8. Answers may vary.

9. Answers may vary.

10. Answers may vary.

11. Answers may vary. Students should have one page written explaining their choice.

(26)

Map Activity

Maps may vary.

(27)

1. United States and Canada are part of North America.

2. The Atlantic Ocean is on the East coast of the United States and Canada.

3. The Pacific Ocean is on the West coast of the United States and Canada.

4. A political map shows cities, states/provinces and national boundaries.

5. Answers may vary.

(28)

EZ✓

1.
a) countries
b) rural
c) flat
d) Rocky
e) Political
f) Topographic

2.
a) TRUE
b) TRUE
c) FALSE
d) TRUE

(31)

3.

Answers may vary.

4.

Answers may vary.

5.

Answers may vary.

6.

Answers may vary.

7.

Answers may vary.

8.

A political map shows cities, towns, states or provinces, nations, and other political boundaries.

9.

A topographic map is a small scale map that shows physical features such as elevation.

10.

A choropleth map uses color to display statistical data such as population or weather.

11.

Answers may vary. Check to make sure the capital cities are correct.

32

Map Activity

Maps may vary. Maps should be of a country with state/provinces labeled, and should include great lakes, oceans, one major river, a mountain range, a title, compass rose, date, author, legend, a grid, coordinates, and surrounding areas.

33

1.

a) **B**

b) **A**

c) **C**

d) **A**

e) **C**

34

1.

a) massive areas

b) four (4)

c) Antarctica

d) Southern
e) seventy (70)

f) Africa

g) Antarctica
h) Australia

i) culturally

j) 195

k) changes

l) diverse place

m) Africa

n) conserve

37

2.

Answers may vary. United States, Canada, Mexico, Caribbean.

3.

Answers may vary. South Africa, Egypt, Morocco, Madagascar, etc.

4.

Answers may vary.

5.

Answers may vary. Maps should accurately show the different classifications of temperature.

38

Map Activity

The 7 continents, 4 oceans, United States, Canada, Mexico and Greenland should be correctly labeled.

39

EZ✓

Word Search Answers

Across

3. choropleth

4. steep

6. scale

8. prime meridian

11. author

12. title

13. sea level

Down

1. latitude

2. compass rose

5. cardinal

7. community

9. amenities

10. todalsigs

40

c	o	m	p	a	s	s	r	o	s	e	l	e	g	e	n	d	m
s	l	o	o	u	r	b	a	n	e	r	y	t	l	n	u	m	m
e	s	c	e	t	e	r	r	i	t	o	r	y	i	o	p	o	l
r	s	a	o	h	n	a	i	d	i	r	e	m	e	m	i	r	p
t	t	d	o	u	h	v	e	b	c	n	r	t	n	s	s	s	b
c	a	r	d	i	n	a	l	d	i	r	e	c	t	i	o	n	s
d	t	c	l	d	r	t	e	f	e	y	r	a	d	n	u	o	b
e	e	o	u	c	f	e	r	g	r	g	s	t	k	t	r	r	t
p	q	o	r	i	q	u	i	y	c	o	n	t	i	n	e	n	t
u	u	r	y	h	e	e	r	p	o	l	i	t	i	c	a	l	l
e	a	d	t	p	c	s	a	w	l	o	y	t	i	n	e	m	a
c	t	i	i	a	u	s	e	r	l	c	a	p	i	t	a	l	u
n	o	n	n	r	l	t	a	a	h	v	k	j	y	u	u	e	d
i	r	a	u	g	t	o	r	u	l	h	l	l	p	j	l	d	a
v	u	t	m	o	u	u	d	t	n	e	o	m	s	e	k	e	r
o	l	e	m	p	r	v	e	h	l	o	v	e	o	m	e	r	g
r	o	s	o	o	a	q	h	o	a	d	r	e	n	s	j	t	d
p	j	l	c	t	l	r	u	r	t	v	d	e	l	a	c	s	s

41

Part A

1. Compass Rose

2. Scale

3. 5 miles

4. 800 km

5. Title, orientation, date, author, legend, scale, index, grid, surrounding area.

6. Noon.

Part B

1. TRUE

2. FALSE

3. The 7 continents, 4 oceans, Greenland, the United States, and Canada should be labeled.

42

EZ✓

Part C

1. Lines of latitude divide the Earth horizontally into equal sections. Lines of longitude divide the Earth vertically into equal sections.

2. They allow you to communicate where something is easily. They give a reference point that people can use to find places.

3. Political maps communicate political boundaries such as cities, towns and states, and are on a large scale. Topographic maps are on a small scale and tell us about physical things such as elevation.

4. Urban communities have a lot of people in an area, have schools, hospitals, libraries and other amenities. Rural communities have fewer people and they are more spread out. They also are set in the countryside outside of cities and tend to have fewer amenities.

5. The world contains seven continents, which are massive areas of land, four oceans and numerous seas. Some scientists consider the area around Antarctica, to be the 5th ocean, which is known as the Southern Ocean. Seventy percent of the earth's surface is covered by water. The world is a very diverse place and people live very differently in the many places of the world. There are 195 countries in the world.

43

Time Zones

-11 -10 -9 -8 -7 -6 -5 -4 -3 -2 -1 0 +1 +2 +3 +4 +5 +6 +7 +8 +9 +10 +11 +12
+12:30
+9:30
+8:30
+6:30
+4:30
+3:30
-3:30
-9:30

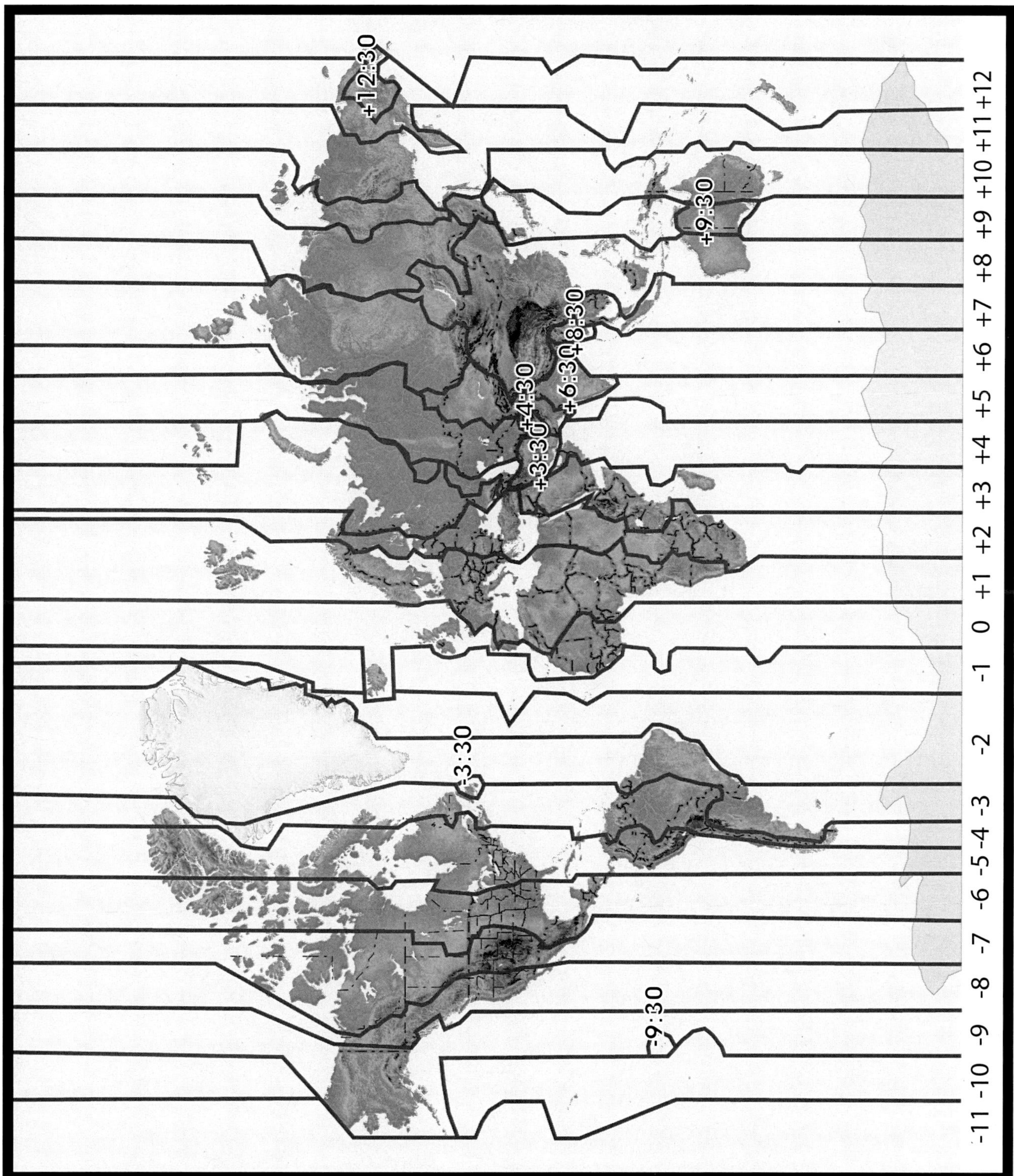

NAME: ______________________________

Choropleth Map

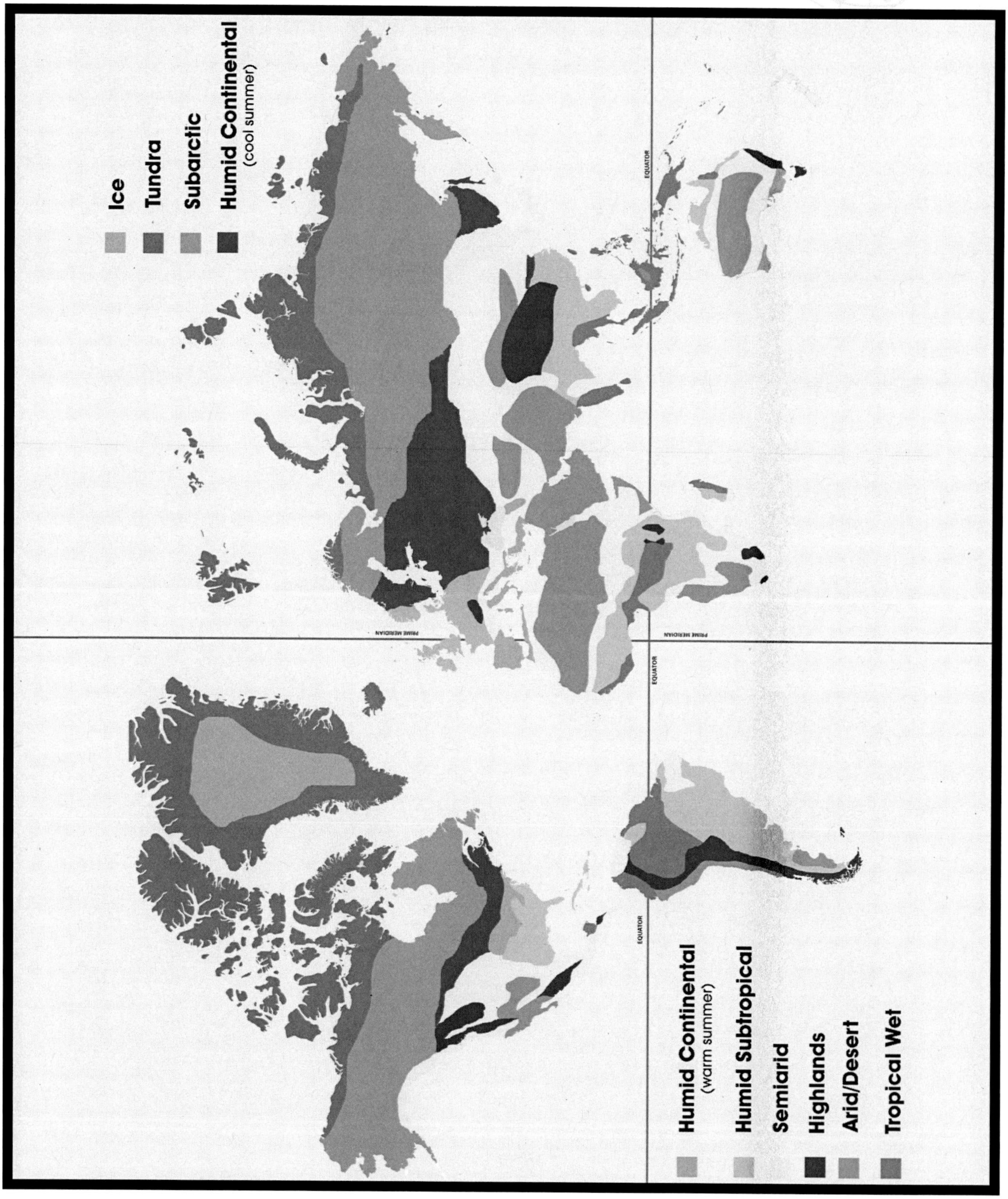

Ice
Tundra
Subarctic
Humid Continental (cool summer)

Humid Continental (warm summer)
Humid Subtropical
Semiarid
Highlands
Arid/Desert
Tropical Wet

EQUATOR
PRIME MERIDIAN

NAME: ______________________

Topographic Map

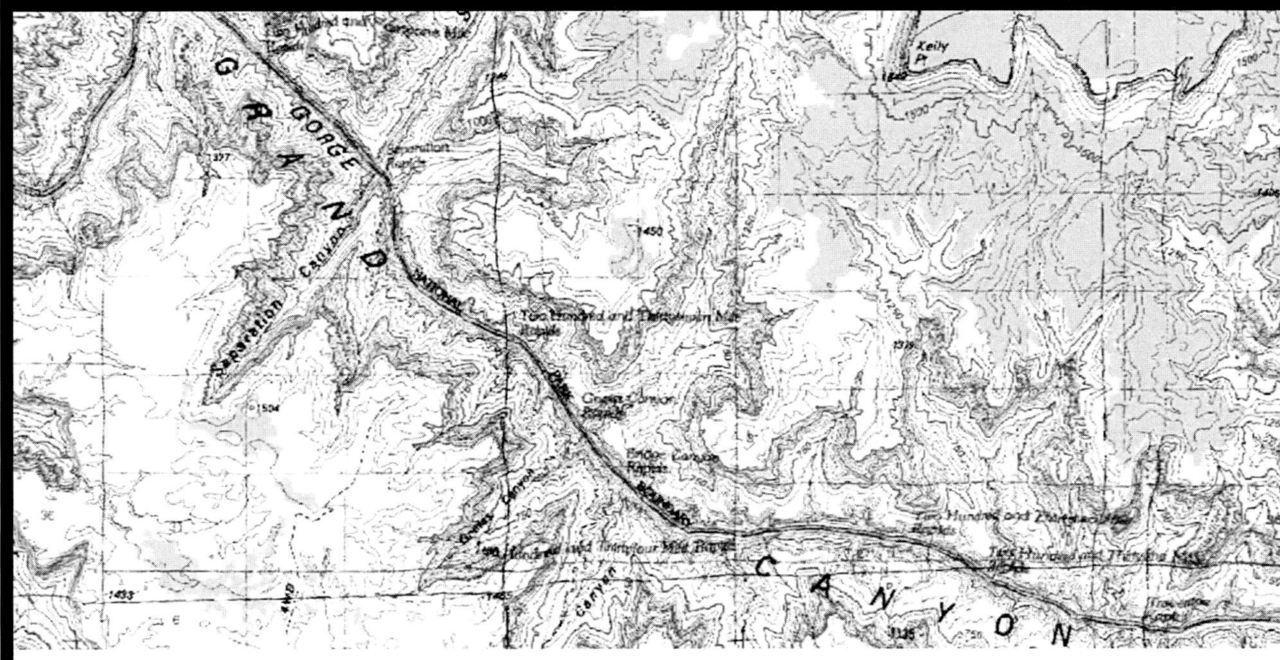

A Topographic Map of the Grand Canyon in Arizona

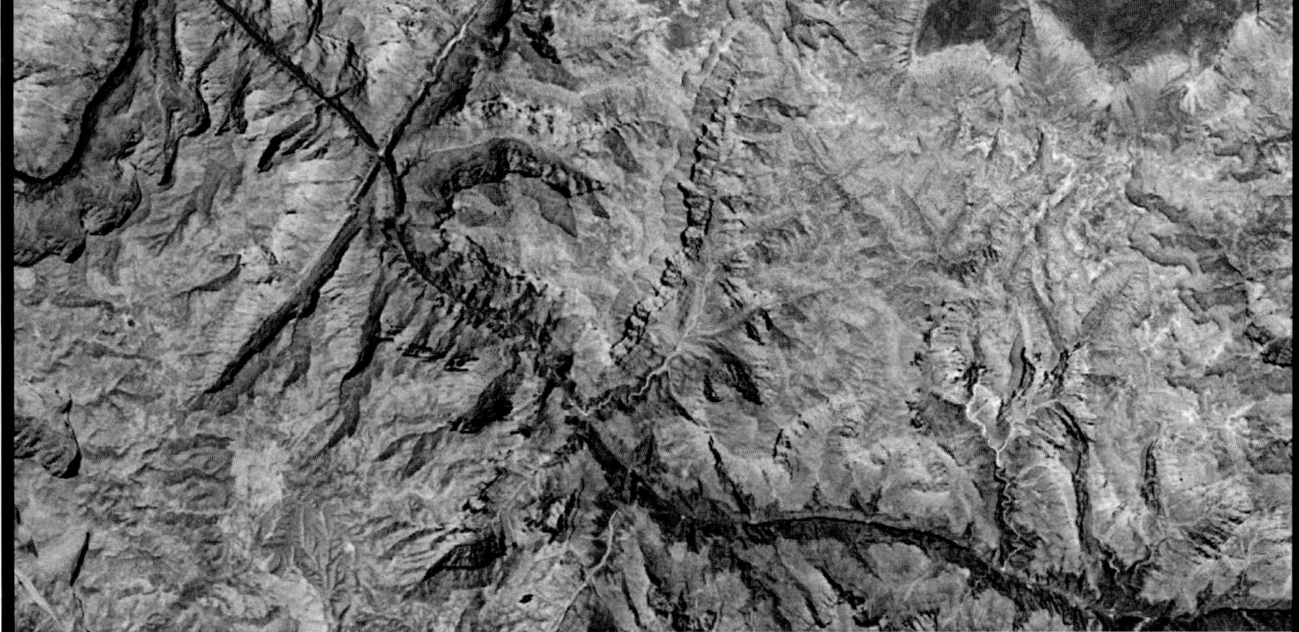

A Satellite Map of the Grand Canyon in Arizona

NAME: ______________________________

Rural and Urban Communities

Urban Map

Rural Map

NAME: ________________________________

North America

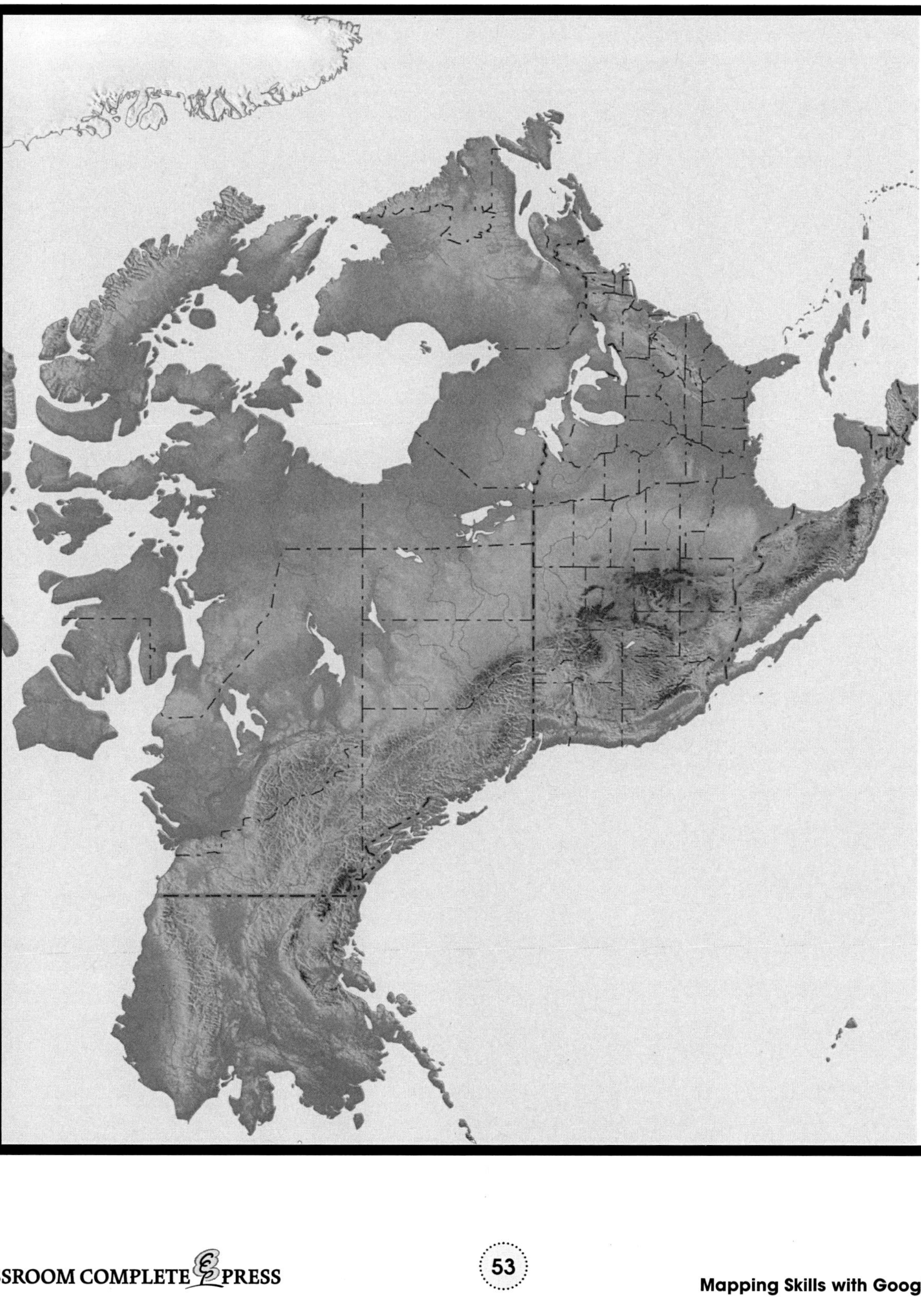

Label the states, provinces, territories and capital cities on the map of North America above. Also label the Great Lakes, Rocky Mountains and the Appalachian Mountains.

NAME: ______________________________

World Continents and Oceans

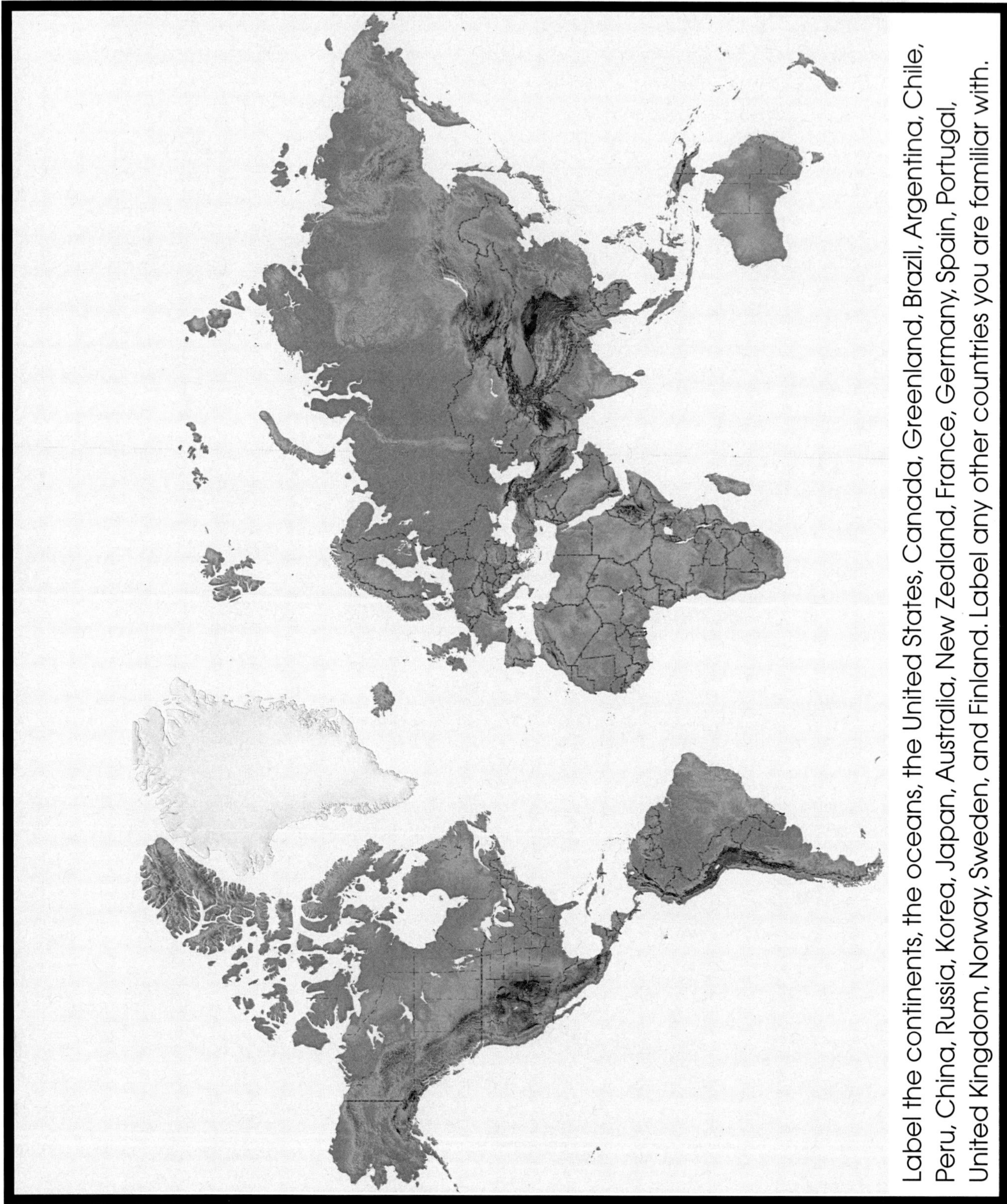

Label the continents, the oceans, the United States, Canada, Greenland, Brazil, Argentina, Chile, Peru, China, Russia, Korea, Japan, Australia, New Zealand, France, Germany, Spain, Portugal, United Kingdom, Norway, Sweden, and Finland. Label any other countries you are familiar with.

Time Zones

-11 -10 -9 -8 -7 -6 -5 -4 -3 -2 -1 0 +1 +2 +3 +4 +5 +6 +7 +8 +9 +10 +11 +12
+12:30
+9:30
+8:30
+6:30
+4:30
+3:30
-3:30
-9:30

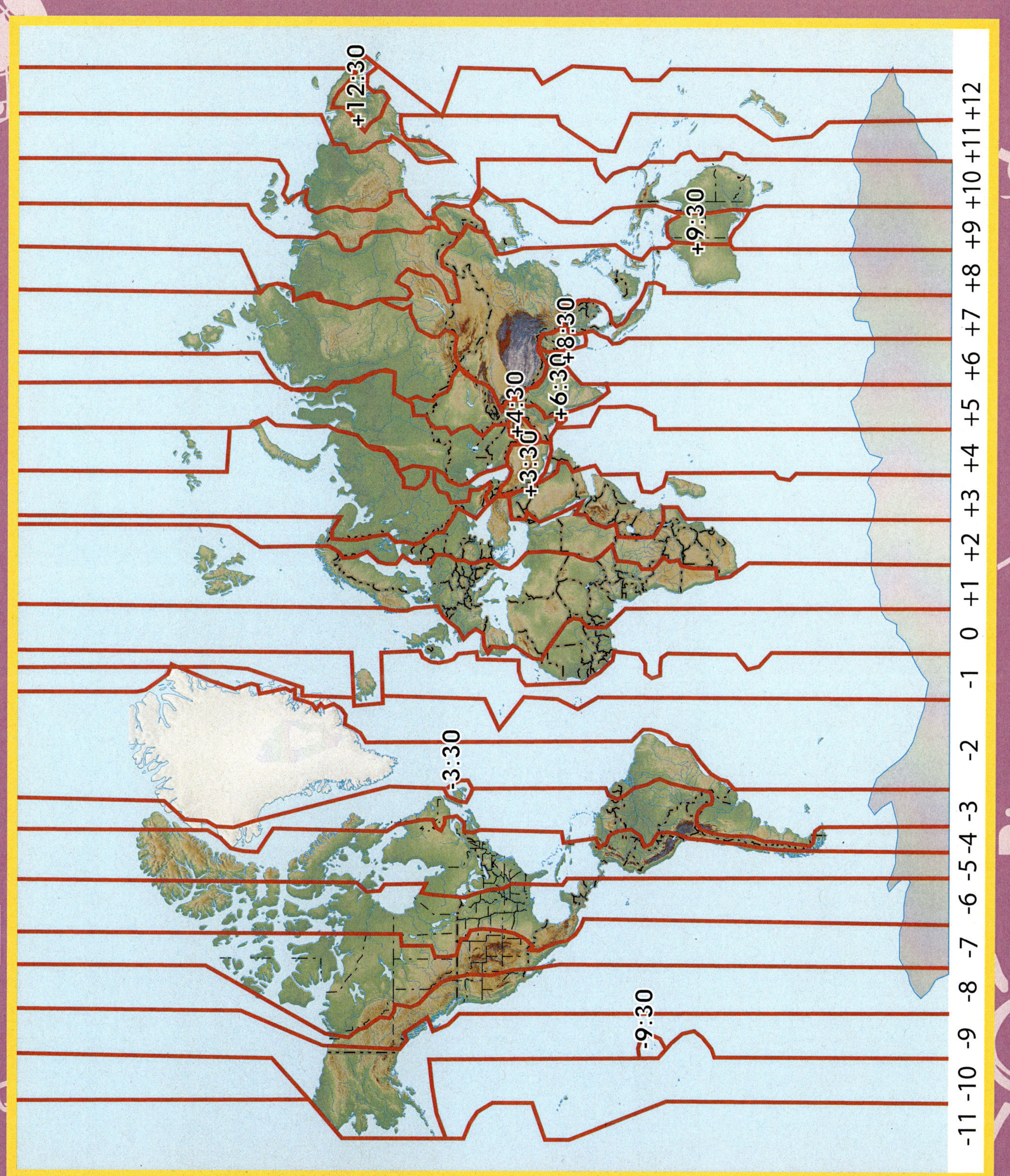

Choropleth Map

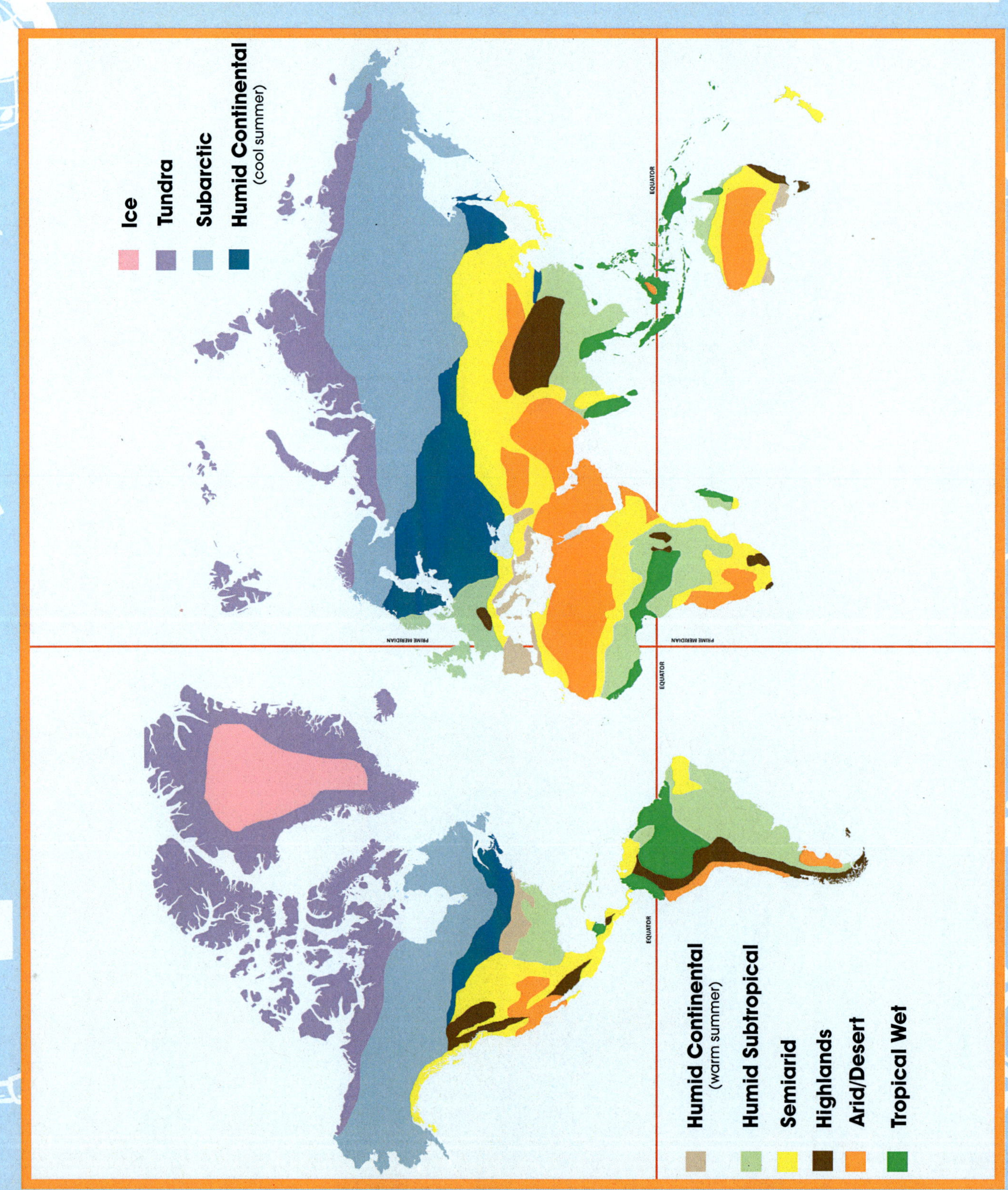

Topographic Map

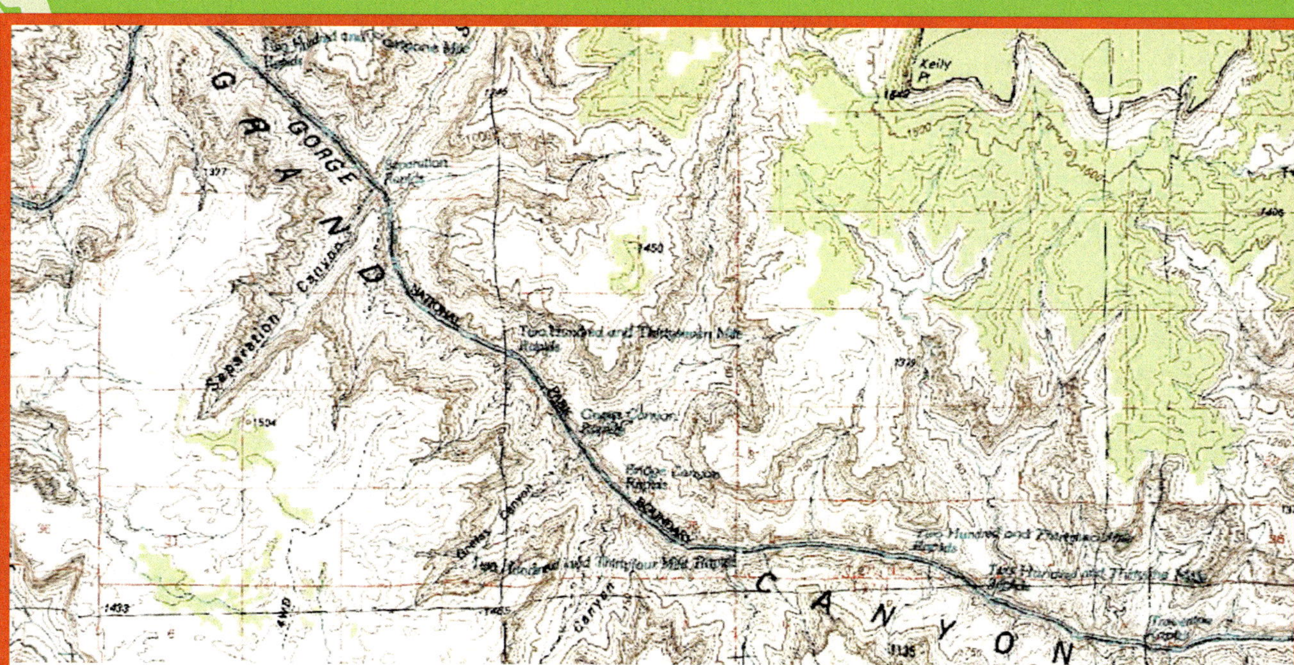

A Topographic Map of the Grand Canyon in Arizona

A Satellite Map of the Grand Canyon in Arizona

Rural and Urban Communities

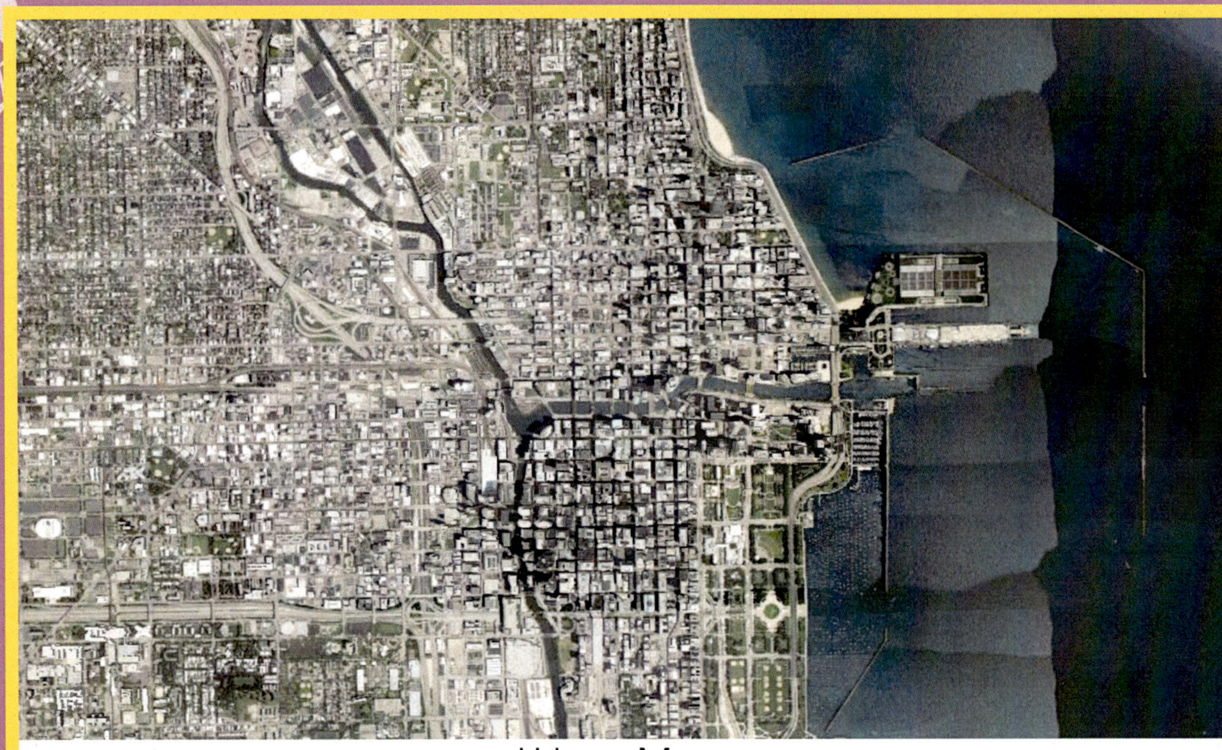

Urban Map

Rural Map

North America

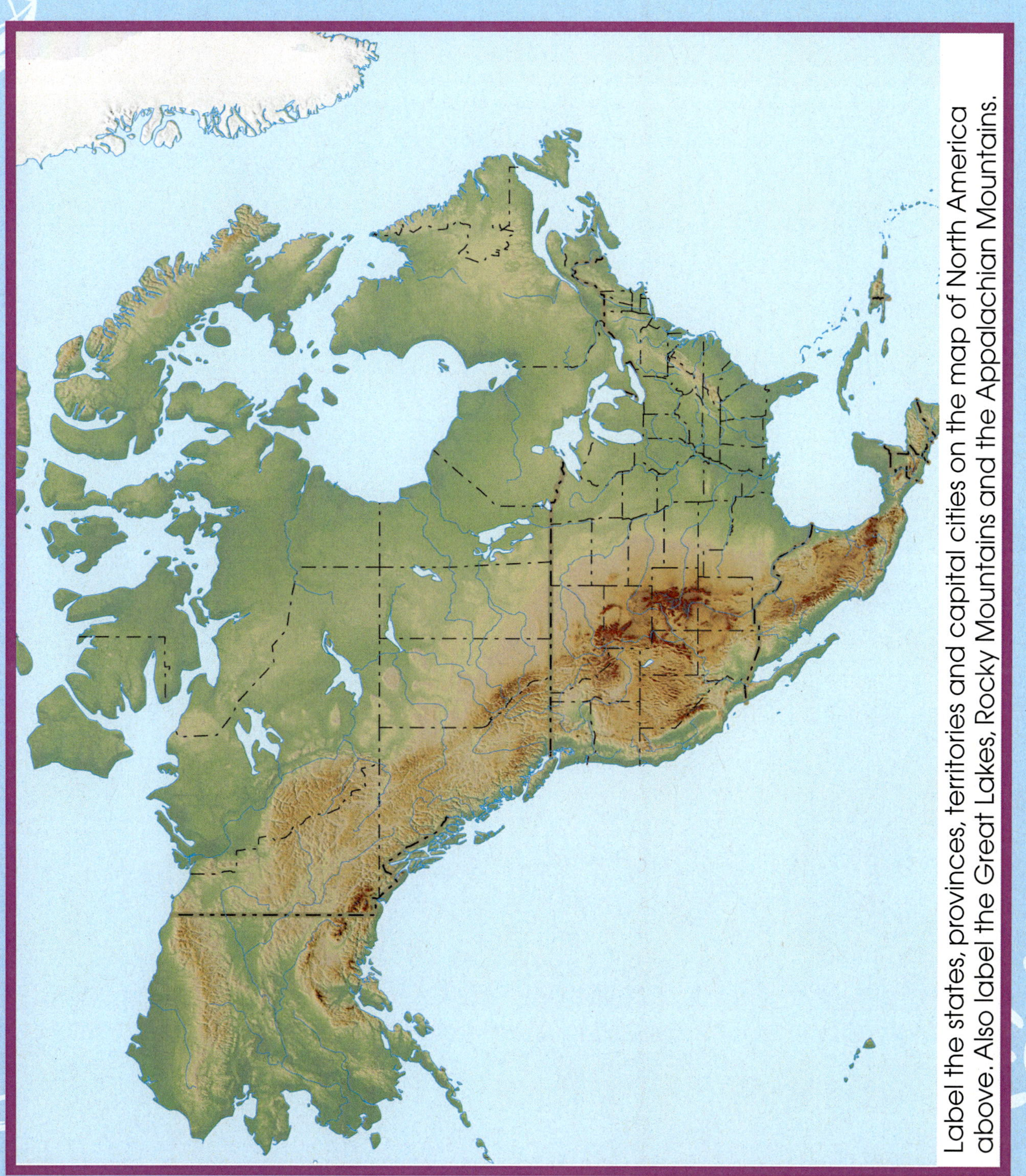

Label the states, provinces, territories and capital cities on the map of North America above. Also label the Great Lakes, Rocky Mountains and the Appalachian Mountains.

World Continents and Oceans

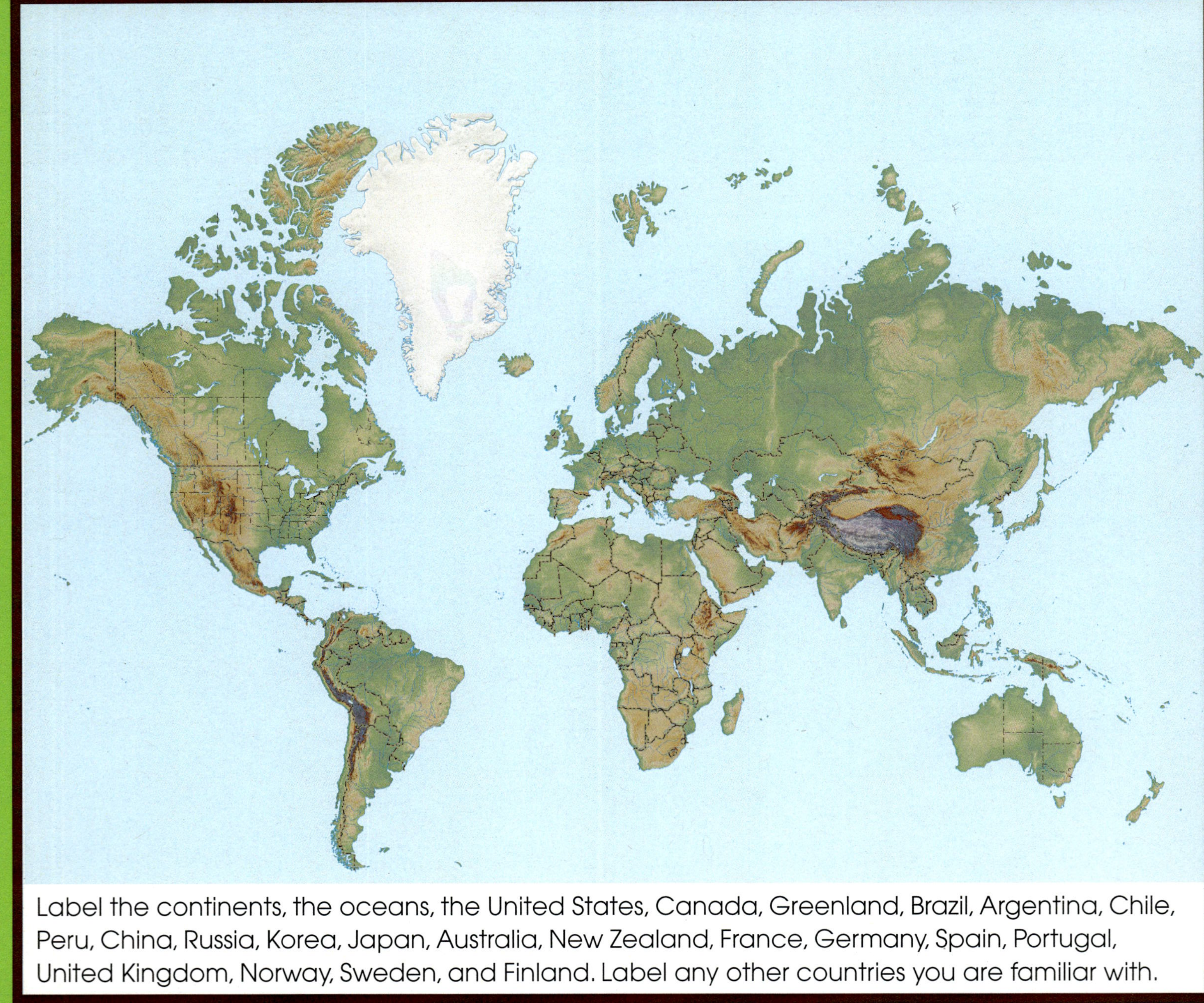

Label the continents, the oceans, the United States, Canada, Greenland, Brazil, Argentina, Chile, Peru, China, Russia, Korea, Japan, Australia, New Zealand, France, Germany, Spain, Portugal, United Kingdom, Norway, Sweden, and Finland. Label any other countries you are familiar with.